WHAT IS IT LIKE

to be parents of a wonderfully bright and adorable little boy—and see him threatened by a fatal disease every day . . .

WHAT IS IT LIKE

to be the doctors and nurses who have that little boy's life in their hands—as they perform an operation they cannot be sure will succeed . . .

WHAT IS IT LIKE

to be that little boy himself—a little boy named Gary Coleman—as so much happened to him so fast, on his amazing journey from death's door to the dizzying heights of life at the summit of stardom . . .

Now they all tell their story in the most inspiring book ever to show you what love and courage really are.

Gary Coleman:
MEDICAL MIRACLE

The Coleman Family & Bill Davidson

BERKLEY BOOKS, NEW YORK

This Berkley book contains the complete
text of the original hardcover edition.
It has been completely reset in a type face
designed for easy reading, and was printed
from new film.

**GARY COLEMAN:
A GIFT OF LIFE**

A Berkley Book / published by arrangement with
Coward, McCann & Geoghegan, Inc.

PRINTING HISTORY
Coward, McCann & Geoghegan edition / October 1981
Berkley edition / October 1982

All rights reserved.
Copyright © 1981 by Sue Coleman, W. G. Coleman,
Gary Coleman and Bill Davidson.
This book may not be reproduced in whole or in part,
by mimeograph or any other means, without permission.
For information address: Coward, McCann & Geoghegan, Inc.,
200 Madison Avenue, New York, New York 10016.

ISBN: 0-425-05595-7

A BERKLEY BOOK ® TM 757,375
Berkley Books are published by Berkley Publishing Corporation,
200 Madison Avenue, New York, New York 10016.
The name "BERKLEY" and the stylized "B" with design
are trademarks belonging to Berkley Publishing Corporation.
PRINTED IN THE UNITED STATES OF AMERICA

Introduction

How do you write a biography of a thirteen-year-old? A successful young comedian once turned down a book about himself, on the grounds that "no one has accomplished enough to make him worth reading about until he's at least fifty."

Even Little Orphan Annie was thirteen for fifty years before her life story made it to Broadway.

But Gary Coleman is the rare exception. *This* thirteen-year-old has packed more drama into his short span of existence than most of us do into middle age. In addition to unexpectedly becoming the entertainment world's most famous child star since Shirley Temple, with his movies and his hit TV series *Diff'rent Strokes*, he is a genuine medical miracle.

Young Gary barely escaped death at twenty-two months, lost both kidneys, and then fought a touch-and-go battle to survive a kidney transplant from a white child killed in an auto accident.

His entire life depends on that donated kidney, on the continuing courage, faith, patience and skill of a pair of remarkable parents, whose love story becomes an integral part of this narrative, and on the extraordinary dedication and competence of the doctors and nurses at Children's Memorial Hospital in Chicago, whose unstinting assistance I hereby acknowledge.

BILL DAVIDSON

Gary Coleman:
MEDICAL MIRACLE

1

The persistent ringing of the phone shattered the silence of the little yellow frame bungalow on 31st Street in Zion, Illinois.

It was 10:03 on the morning of December 18, 1973.

Sue Coleman, a handsome, elegant woman, then thirty, heard the phone; she was in the backyard retrieving a Christmas tree stand carelessly left in the snow of the driveway by her five-year-old son, Gary.

Sue was at home alone, having just finished her night-shift as a Licensed Practical Nurse at Victory Memorial Hospital in nearby Waukegan. She feared morning telephone calls; too many of them lately had meant bad news. She hurried into the neat pine-paneled kitchen and answered, only to freeze at the sound of the voice. It was Dr. Casimir Firlit at Children's Memorial Hospital in Chicago, some fifty miles away.

Dr. Firlit was jovial, as usual, but there was an uncharacteristic briskness to his opening amenities, and he soon got to the point. "Sue," he said, "you'll have to bring Gary down here to the hospital as quickly as possible today. We may have a kidney for him."

Sue went numb. She had been expecting this call, or one with a slightly different meaning, since before Thanksgiving, but still she was unprepared for it. "You mean? . . . the donor? . . . some other poor child? . . . dead?"

"I can't tell you any more," said the doctor. "I'll be able to give you the details when you get here with Gary. How soon?"

"I guess about two or three this afternoon. I have to pick up Willie at work. Then we have to get Gary out of school. Then . . ."

Dr. Firlit's voice softened. "Just make it as quickly as you can," he said, "and please try not to worry. We'll see you some time this afternoon."

Sue hung up unaware she hadn't even said goodbye. As she later recalled it, she felt nothing, once the shock of the unexpected call had passed. Not dread, not panic, not gratitude.

For four years, she had sublimated her anxieties, throwing all her energies into acting as the nurse on her own son's case. She had administered his daily medications, and washed hundreds of thousands of diapers, urine-soaked from the surgically-created bypass opening in Gary's side. She had helped the little boy survive near-fatal uremic poisoning, the total loss of his right kidney, the steady deterioration of the remaining left one.

As a nurse, she realized that Gary must now face

the most crucial procedure of all. As a mother, she couldn't prevent a brief regret: Why couldn't this have waited until after Gary's Christmas?

The moment came and went and Sue was the cool, collected nurse once again. She phoned her husband, Willie, at the Abbott Pharmaceutical laboratories where he delivered chemicals and biological substances to scientists working on drug experimentation in the lab, and gave him Dr. Firlit's news. Big, strong Willie, always in control, yet she could detect immediate concern. "Not the dialysis machine?" he asked. "No," said Sue, "from the way Dr. Firlit sounded, I think it's the real thing—a transplant. I'll be over to pick you up in about twenty minutes."

Sue sat down at the kitchen table and hastily composed a note to Gary's principal, Robert Fink, explaining why Gary had to be excused from class. Then she put on a warm quilted coat and drove off in the family's 1965 Chevrolet. She headed down Sheridan Road to the Abbott research facility in north Chicago. Willie was waiting for her outside the glass-enclosed reception building. He had thrown a coat over his white uniform.

Willie kissed Sue tenderly and slipped into the driver's seat. He always drove the car on the hundreds of trips Gary had made to the hospital in Chicago. As he said repeatedly, "I'd never risk Sue behind the wheel in that crazy traffic down there."

Willie, six feet tall and powerfully built, gripped the wheel tightly as they headed north to Gary's school in Zion. His face glistened with a thin film of sweat, even though the temperature outside was only thirty-five degrees and the aging car's heater was not working too well. He squeezed Sue's hand. "Let's just cool it," he said. "I had a dream that Gary had this operation and he turned out fine." Sue smiled wanly and patted Willie's arm.

They reached the Shiloh Park Elementary School at 11:26 A.M. Sue went inside to the principal's office with her note, and a few minutes later, Gary came cheerfully out of his kindergarten class. At that age, the kidney problems had not yet impeded his growth significantly and he looked like any other normal five-and-a-half-year-old in a red snowsuit. He was a miniature replica of his father, with the same round face, medium-brown skin and tightly-curled black hair.

Gary

I sure was surprised to see Mom. She never came to the school except when it was time to pick me up, or if I was in trouble with Mr. Fink because I punched out some big kid who was pickin' on me.

There wasn't any trouble that day. I was having fun. We were cutting out paper Christmas trees and things like that to paste up on the windows, and then we were going to rehearse the Christmas play. So I was a little bugged when the monitor came in from Mr. Fink's office and said my mom was waiting outside for me in the hall. Then I got excited. I remembered that I had picked out a new toy train for my Christmas

A GIFT OF LIFE

present down at the Magnus-Wheel Travel Hobby Store. Probably Mom was taking me to get it before the store closed. But that was silly—the store didn't close until nine o'clock at night. Maybe they were running out of the SD-40 Diesel I wanted and Mom didn't want me to miss out on it.

I found her in the hall and said, "What's up, Mom? Whatever it is, let's get it over with. I've got to get back to class because we're rehearsing the Christmas play today."

Mom tried to say something but she couldn't. She grabbed me up and held me in her arms. She was kinda sobbing. It didn't look good for what I had in mind, but I tried anyway. I said, "I know. I bet we're going to Magnus to get that train I picked out for my present."

Mom put me down and said, "No, Gary, we have to go to the hospital."

I said, "Not *again*. If it's only that dumb dialysis machine, why can't it wait until tomorrow, when we're through rehearsing? Besides, we're also gonna do a Chanukah pageant."

Mom said, "It isn't the dialysis machine. It may be the real thing—the transplant."

She didn't have to tell me any more. I was only a little kid of five at the time but I knew exactly what she was talking about. I just wished that Mom and Dad didn't worry so much. I didn't *feel* sick. It wasn't like I was having a heart attack or something.

I said, "OK, then, but I'm starved. Can we have something to eat first before we go to the hospital?"

Mom said, "No eating. If it's going to be an operation, your stomach should be empty. But there is one thing you should do. It's a long drive. Go into the little boys' room and do your pee-pee."

I went to the toilet down the hall and did like I had been doing for about a year and a half. I went into a stall where the other kids couldn't see me, and I opened my pants to get at my pouch. The pouch was made out of plastic and the top of it was glued over a hole in my belly. The bottom of the pouch was kind of a valve that unscrewed. I unscrewed the valve and all the urine that had collected in the pouch drained out into the toilet. I couldn't pee through my penis, but none of the other kids in the school knew it.

I screwed up the valve again, closed my pants and went back to where Mom was waiting in the hall.

I said, "OK, Mom, let's go to Chicago and get it over with."

The drive into Chicago was a long and arduous one. It was cold and no one felt much like talking. Willie took a series of zigzagging short cuts to the Tri-State Tollway and then sped south on the eight-lane Interstate. Traffic was light at that time of day, except for the normal procession of trucks carrying goods and food from Milwaukee to Chicago. As the Colemans passed the Howard Johnson Oasis—a usual stop for them—Gary once again requested a lunch break and once again was gently dissuaded by his mother.

Just below Highland Park, the Tri-State fed into

the Edens Expressway. The Chicago-area traffic thickened. It was stop-and-go for a while until they passed the O'Hare Airport turnoff. Then, suddenly, the Chicago skyline appeared on the horizon. Willie exited at Fullerton Avenue and headed west toward Lake Michigan. A few minutes later, they were in front of the modern red-brick building that is Children's Memorial Hospital, a part of the Northwestern University Medical Center complex. Willie drove into the emergency entrance.

It was 2:47 P.M.

Sue

We got Gary admitted and rushed him up to the fifth floor. That's where all the surgery is done and where they treat the children who are kidney patients. There was a lot of quiet bustle and I got the feeling that they were all waiting for Gary. There was also an air of excitement on the floor. They still didn't do that many kidney transplants on children in those days.

Some nurses took Gary away to show him all the space-age-type equipment in the intensive care area. Willie and I were told to see Dr. Firlit in his office. Dr. Peter Lewy was with him; Dr. Lewy had been Gary's nephrologist for years. It was a cramped little office and there was barely room for the four of us.

Dr. Firlit did most of the talking. I guess he had

just finished surgery because he was still wearing his light green suit and cap. The funny things you remember: I thought how well the colors set off his pale skin and blond mustache.

Dr. Firlit said, "Well, I figure you've guessed by now, but we *do* have the kidney. A pair of them, in fact, from the same boy. The tissue-typing went through the central computer and we got them both. The computer said that Gary and another little boy here, Chandel, were the closest match in the entire Midwest."

I caught my breath, thinking of the youngster who had to have died in order to have both kidneys donated. I thought of the agony *his* mother must be going through. I said, "Can you tell me about him, the little boy who died, I mean?"

Dr. Firlit said, "Sue, the ethics of the situation, even the law, is that total anonymity must be preserved. All I can tell you is that he was six years old and that it was an automobile accident. He died yesterday."

I could see that Willie was alarmed. "Yesterday?" he said. "But the kidney..."

"It was removed immediately and it's being cooled and nourished in a special device we have," Dr. Lewy explained. "The kidney can be kept alive, in a sense, for up to ninety-six hours."

There was a moment's silence as Dr. Firlit just looked at us as if he didn't know how to begin. Finally he said, "Sue and Willie, you have a very important decision to make—maybe the most important in your lives. You have to decide whether or not to give us permission to go ahead with the transplant."

"What are the choices?" Willie asked.

Dr. Firlit said, "First, we can do nothing. If so, Gary will die. I know he's been running around and going to school normally, even with that urine pouch, but as I told you in November, the function of his remaining kidney is down to about five percent of normal. That's just about the danger point, and as you know, people can't live without kidneys any more than they can without a heart.

"The second choice is to put Gary on dialysis, which is what I thought we'd have to do originally, since we usually have to wait a long time until a donated kidney comes along. On dialysis, Gary would have to come here three times a week. A vein and an artery in his arm will be hooked up to a machine for six to eight hours, while the machine cleans his entire blood supply of poisons, the way a kidney normally does. At the present state of the art, he'll be debilitated and restricted in getting around, but the machine will keep him alive and functioning. The only problem is that until a new federal program gets into full swing, there may not be enough machines to go around.

"The third choice is the transplant. But there are risks involved there, too."

I sucked in my breath, and I heard Willie do the same. "Doctor," Willie said, "tell us about the risks and don't hold anything back."

"All right," said Dr. Firlit. "The greatest danger is that Gary's body might reject the organ, attacking it as if it were a foreign invader like a disease bacteria. Rejection could take place immediately and we'd have to remove the kidney. If not, the next ten days are critical in terms of rejection. If the kidney gets through that, we keep hoping and praying, for six months. Beyond that stage, the chances improve until the second year. After two years without rejection, we figure we've got it made. There are exceptions, of course, but usually, then, there is only chronic *slow* rejection, which we can manage. As to the odds, I think Gary has a better than fifty-percent chance of making it all the way."

Trembling, I took Willie's arm. Willie said, "Do you mind if Sue and I talk it over for a few minutes?"

"Not at all," said Dr. Lewy, and he and Dr. Firlit went outside into the surgeons' lounge.

Dr. Lewy and Dr. Firlit are both young men, but they had been around long enough to remember the time, less than a decade before, when neither transplants nor dialysis were available for young children with kidney deficiencies. Dr. Firlit later recalled that that's exactly what he was thinking about while he paced the surgeons' lounge, waiting for Sue and Willie Coleman to make up their minds: "The children, in those days, simply came to the hospitals to die a horrible death. Transplantation was considered impractical for the young and the few dialysis machines were reserved for older patients, as they still are in England. So the children were puffed up with uremia. They had huge distended bellies. They were in severe pain and itched uncontrollably. They scratched constantly. They turned green. They reeked of urine no matter how often they were cleaned up. The urine exuded through the skin and even formed a frost of crystals on the upper lip, like some hideous white mustache. And then, in agony, they died."

Willie

As we sat in Dr. Firlit's office, I had pretty much made up my mind that we had to go ahead with the transplant. But I could see that Sue was still troubled in her mind.

I said, "Sue, honey, if we think about it calmly, there really isn't any other choice. Either we take a chance on Gary making it through the surgery and the rejection problems, and at least having a possible chance of being OK for the rest of his life, or we don't have the surgery and he gets very sick and goes on dialysis, and maybe doesn't make it at all."

Sue said, "Tell me again about that dream you had."

I said, "I think it was God showing me the way because I saw this room we're sitting in. Every detail. And you know I've never been in here before. I saw us talking, the way we are now. I saw Gary going into the operating room. Then I saw him coming home, happy as could be. And he was running around and laughing and playing, as usual. And he was OK."

Sue said, "Thanks, Willie, that's just the spark of faith I needed. Go out and tell the doctors we've made up our minds to go ahead." So I went out and told them. Dr. Firlit came in and talked to us for a while.

Dr. Lewy left to prepare Gary for surgery.

Gary

This hospital was my old stompin' grounds and I was having a lot of fun before Dr. Lewy came in. The nurses are all neat ladies there, especially Toni Greenslade. She showed me places in the hospital I'd never seen before. There was the Intensive Care Unit, where she said I might end up later that day. Man, it was exciting. There were machines, with TV screens, all over the place. There were little green lights running across the screens. There was lots of other machines with lights on them, too. It was like I was in Houston Mission Control for a space shot. Also, there were kids in bed with plastic bubbles over their heads. They looked just like space helmets. Miss Greenslade told me that was a new way to give patients oxygen, *just* like in space.

Then Dr. Lewy came in and it was the same old stuff with the nurses, like when I'd been in for operations before. I was starving and I kept asking them for food, but they wouldn't give me any.

Not even a drink of water. Instead, they gave me an enema. When I was through going to the bathroom, they put me in bed and scrubbed my tummy.

Then Mom and Dad came in. Mom looked like she had been crying. Dad told me what I already knew—that they were going to do the transplant. I said, "Well, if we're gonna do it, let's get on with it." I was a little scared but I tried to act like it didn't bother me at all, so they wouldn't worry. That seemed to cheer Mom up a lot.

After that, the nurses came in again and they pulled a dirty trick on me. They gave me a balloon to play with. I blew it up and was having a lot of fun with it, but when I sucked in some of the air in the balloon, my head began to spin around. Just before I passed out altogether, I figured they had slipped me a little anesthetic in that balloon.

Gary was taken into the operating room at 6:48 P.M. At about the same time, Sue and Willie were escorted to a waiting room just outside the Intensive Care Unit, which they could view through large plate glass windows.

Other parents were in the waiting room. There was a woman whose son had suffered severe burns over most of his body. There was a young couple from Iowa whose little daughter was undergoing heart surgery. There was an Oriental couple whose child was being treated for a rare lung disease. The parents sat on the chrome and plastic waiting-room chairs or tried to get some sleep on cots brought in by the hospital's housekeeping department.

Sue

With all my anxiety, being in that waiting room was one of the most inspiring and heartwarming experiences of my life. With all *their* worries, the other parents went out of their way to be kind to us. Most of all, I remember the woman whose son was so badly burned and obviously dying.

To this day, all I know about her is that her husband was a policeman. But what she did was almost unbelievable. *She* was the one whose spirits constantly were up and she kept everyone else's courage up too. She knew that the chances of her child living were slim and I think her cheerfulness was her way of maintaining herself. She seemed to be wanting to make sure that the rest of us didn't take on added depression from her own.

She was a very brave lady. Once an hour she'd go in to see her little boy in Intensive Care and she'd come out and we could tell she was hurting. But she'd say, "Okay, now what are we going to talk about?" I admire people with that ability to hide their own grief in an effort to help others.

But in the very beginning, in the first hour that Gary was in surgery, I felt that I needed a different kind of help. Willie had worked overtime the day before and he was so exhausted that he was dozing off. Without even telling him where I was going, I just left. The other people, I guess, thought I was heading for the ladies' room. Instead, I took the elevator to the arcade floor. Just across the hall from the coffee shop, I found the chapel.

It was a welcoming room, warm and simple, with wood paneling and a statue of the Virgin Mary. No one else was there. I sat down in a pew and I must have been alone in the chapel, praying and thinking, for about twenty minutes.

As a young girl in the South, I had been raised as a Methodist, but I was no longer a regular churchgoer. Yet, I never felt closer to God than I did during those moments in the hospital chapel. I said to Him, "I need to sort things out in my mind. I have to bring myself down to where I can say, 'Look, it's necessary, it has to be done. Either way, I have to accept it.' "

And then, after a while, it came to me. I said, "Okay, either way it goes, I *do* accept it. I don't want my son to die, but if he does, then I know there must be a reason. Lord, it's up to you." And I felt better. I really did. I had admitted to myself that if that was the way God wanted it, there was nothing I could do about it. And that if God had a reason to keep Gary alive, I would accept that, too, and try to be worthy of the gift. I guess I had blocked out of my mind the possibility that Gary might *not* make it, but now that I had put it in God's hands, I could live with it.

I cried. Then I went across the hall and got some coffee. I went back upstairs and told Willie I had been in the chapel. He took my hand and I felt peace.

I settled down on a cot, but I couldn't sleep. Instead, I spent the next couple of hours thinking way back—to how it all started with Willie and me and Gary.

2

The Gary Coleman story began long before his conception in North Chicago, Illinois. The young man stems from deep and powerful roots—both genetic and geographic.

Gary

Two of the best television shows I ever saw were *Roots* and *Roots II*. I enjoyed the African stuff where they took slaves and all, but the part I liked best was after the Civil War, when Kunta Kinte's people were living in the South in the United States. It reminded me of the stories I used to

A GIFT OF LIFE 17

hear from Mom and Dad and my grandpa and two grandmas about when they were growing up in the South. Not that it was slavery, of course, but a lot of things reminded me about what happened to the people in *Roots* later on. I specially used to listen to the stories Grandpa told me when we were out fishin' or just foolin' around. Grandpa and my mom lived just across the river from the part of Tennessee where Alex Haley and his folks grew up.

Sue and Willie were both born and raised in the rural South at a time when being black, in that region, was not beautiful. It was the World War II period, and the devastating echoes of slavery and Reconstruction were still heard. Rural blacks were still mainly confined to the old plantations as tenant farmers; night riders still occasionally took to the back roads to keep them in their place. It was more than two decades before a Constitutional amendment would abolish the poll tax and allow them to vote. Segregated schools were the norm; most black children received only the rudiments of education from ill-equipped teachers in ramshackle buildings. Decent health facilities for blacks were only beginning to emerge through federal legislation. States Righters still dominated Southern legislatures.

In World War II the armed forces were segregated and blacks were mainly assigned the housekeeping and grave-digging chores in their own units, under white officers. The more adventurous of the Southern blacks fled north to comparatively well-paying defense-factory jobs in Detroit and elsewhere, but even there they might be caught up in devastating race riots.

Against this background, Willie and Sue separately moved north in the postwar 1950s; both were barely in their teens. Later, with perseverance, courage, intelligence and devotion to one another, both beat the odds by bursting the shackles of the menial jobs to which Southern blacks were traditionally relegated and moved to new levels of dignity as highly-respected paraprofessionals in the health field.

These were the genes young Gary Coleman inherited to aid him in his own stubborn struggle for survival.

Of his two parents, his father had by far the rougher time.

Willie was born in Yazoo City, Mississippi, in 1939, the fourth youngest of thirteen children of Albert and Luretha Coleman. To this day, he resents the fact that his parents apparently ran out of names by the time he came along. He is listed on his birth certificate with just the initials W. G., and that is what his mother (a proud lady who resembles and sounds like Pearl Bailey) still calls him. The name Willie was assigned him later by an employer. There was already a brother named Willie in the family when W. G. was born. W. G. justifiably lamented, "Why can't I have a *real* name like everybody else?"

He had plenty of other things to lament when he was a child. His family were sharecroppers on three different farms in the vicinity of Belzoni, Mississippi, planting, picking and chopping cotton in what Luretha Coleman, now widowed, describes as "the hardest work any human being ever had to do for the least money." Her son most clearly remembers the third of the three farms, the Bill Ellison plantation.

Willie

There was nine of us living in a sorry little house on the plantation—my mother, my father, and those of my brothers and sisters who didn't move away or die as little babies. Right after breakfast, we all had to go out in the fields to pick and chop cotton. It doesn't seem like no end to it, especially if you're doing it for someone else. If we picked fifteen bales—a thousand pounds in a bale—seven and a half bales went to The Man, Mr. Ellison. He was seventy years old and about to sell out the plantation for a housing development, but that didn't matter to him. For every bale we picked, we got a hundred dollars but he got seven hundred. We were supposed to get half.

You didn't dispute The Man. He'd say, "Take the tractor and load your bales into three trailers and haul them to the cotton gin. I don't want you to stop nowhere until you get back. You give the receipt to me and *I'm* going to collect for the cotton." So we never knew what the price of cotton was, and The Man could say it was two hundred dollars and give us a hundred when it really was eight hundred dollars a bale and he kept seven.

Not only that, but we were always in debt to The Man. You'd go to the feed store and get so many pounds of cotton seed, and you'd say "Put it on my cuff." You didn't *have* to buy it that way, but that's the way it was done. It's how The Man wanted it. It was the same with groceries, and even if you went outside to buy furniture or a car, the debt was turned over to The Man to collect. So if he said it was OK, you could go out and buy a used car for four hundred dollars, and then he'd assume the debt and you'd be paying him—not the person you bought it from—for ten years. With interest, you'd end up paying him maybe three thousand dollars for that four hundred dollar secondhand car.

Even as a kid, I argued against this, but that's the way my father and mother always did it. I learned by being beat with an ironing cord that you don't dispute your elders no more than you dispute The Man. So on weekends I'd go out and make money for myself. I'd mow lawns—a dollar fifty for three, four acres—and I set up a shoeshine stand with one of my brothers at the Belzoni courthouse. We got ten cents a shine.

On Saturday night I used my money to go to the movies. My mother would tell me to be outside at ten o'clock so she could drive me home in the family car. But if I paid twenty cents, I wanted to see more than the feature. I'd stay to see Popeye and Woody Woodpecker and my mother would give up and go home, not knowing where I was. Then I'd come out and have to walk four miles along the dark highway. It was dangerous in those days. The white kids had pickup trucks and on Saturday night they'd pile into one with guns, looking for black kids to kill. They never got me, but I had some close calls. A couple of my friends weren't so lucky. One of them ended up in the Mississippi River near Silver City.

My father and mother warned me not to do it, but instead of going to the all-black rural school, I went to school with white kids in Belzoni. It wasn't against the law, like in Georgia, but it's just that the black parents didn't want to cause trouble. None of the kids bothered me. What *did* bother me was that they brought baloney sandwiches on white bread for lunch, and I had to eat a biscuit with molasses. When we went to gym, they had shorts and sneakers, but, winter or summer, I had to strip down to my long underware and high-top work shoes.

I was inhibited by their way of walking, their way of talking, their way of doing things, grouping up, dressing. I would go home and ask *why* I had to be different with my biscuits and molasses and my long underwear. Black parents never listened. They'd say, "That's the way we *always* did it," and I wasn't allowed to argue back. I knew I'd have to break away someday and figure things out for myself.

In 1952, when I was thirteen, something exciting was stirring in our house. One day, my father went to Belzoni and bought eight bus tickets, which he gave to my mother. Then, in the middle of the night, he was gone. My mother said he went to Lima, Ohio, where Ford Motors was building a new plant. A friend of ours who had sneaked away three years before had got a construction job there for my father. I asked my mother why it was necessary to slip away in the middle of the night. My mother said, "That's the way we *always* did it"—between planting seasons, so it would be a long time before The Man came around asking "Where is your husband?" or "Where is your oldest boy?"

I said, "But we don't owe The Man anything— just for that old beat-up car out there. We can leave that. What are we afraid of?" My mother said, "Never you mind."

About a week later, the rest of us left, using the bus tickets my father had bought. We sneaked out in the middle of the night, too, leaving the car behind so The Man wouldn't realize we were gone until planting season. We got to Lima the next day and my father met us. He had been hired on at the Ford plant. We all moved into a little house he had rented in the outskirts.

I was the happiest kid in the world when a school bus came to pick me up. It took me to the Perry Township School. But when I got there it was all-black, and I still had my biscuit and molasses lunch, and I was still wearing my high-top shoes and long underwear.

At the time Willie moved to Ohio with his parents, he didn't even dream of the existence of Edmonia Sue Lovelace, then four years younger at nine, and still living in the South, in Florence, Alabama. Sue's life, though a hard one, had not been as cruel as Willie's.

For one thing, Florence is in the far northwest corner of Alabama, just across the border from Tennessee—the so-called Hill Country of small farmers, where slavery had never gotten the grip it did on the vast plantations of the Black Belt farther south. While discrimination existed in fact, blacks led a much more comfortable life in the Hill Country than they did nearly anywhere else in the region.

The Lovelaces lived on their own farm, which Sue's grandfather had been allowed to purchase in the early 1900s, and while there wasn't much money, the family was at least able to grow its own food:

corn, vegetables, a few hogs and cattle. The Lovelaces, moreover, are extremely light-skinned and were acceptable to their rural white neighbors. Sue's father, Jesse, called Jack, is in his seventies now but still is a dapper, handsome man with a nearly pink complexion and a pencil-line mustache, who strongly resembles the late British actor, Ronald Colman.

Now living in the North in a comfortable house in an integrated neighborhood, Jack fondly recalls his days in Florence. "The white folks," he says, "used to hire me to do odd jobs around their places and to help them bring in the crops. Then, on Saturday nights, we'd all pile into a pickup truck with a lot of beer and go fox-hunting with our dogs across the border in Tennessee. We sat around a campfire and did a lot of drinking and storytelling, and we heard the dogs yelping a lot, but we never caught much in the way of fox."

His only daughter, Sue, does not remember Florence so fondly.

Sue

I was a very lonely little girl. My mother died of breast cancer when I was only a year and a half old. My father was a happy-go-lucky fellow who used to move around a lot whenever we heard of good-paying jobs in other parts of the country. Before I was born, he worked for years as a janitor and cafeteria attendant at the Abbott

Laboratories in North Chicago and only came back to the farm in Florence when my grandfather got sick and died. I had two older brothers who didn't live with us. I was mainly raised by my grandmother, Elizabeth Lovelace, who was over seventy when my mother died and a hundred and two when she passed away a few years ago. I spent most of my childhood wishing I had a sister to talk to.

Florence wasn't so bad, but being in Alabama, I had to go to an all-black school in the Pisgah Methodist Church. Although I sang in the choir, I didn't get much of an education there; segregated schools do not prepare you for the real world. I found it hard to make friends. I was lighter skinned than most of the girls, and I guess that turned them off. What a shame that we still had that hangover from slavery when dark-skinned blacks didn't like light-skinned blacks, and vice versa.

When I was eight, my father married again. Mary is dark-skinned, and some in our family were not too happy about Dad's new bride. At first, I didn't get along with her either, but for other reasons. As Mary explained it later, I was jealous of my handsome dashing father and I didn't want to share his affections with anyone. She said she had the same problem with my grandmother.

But Mary is a lovely, bright woman who used some very clever strategies to win me over. She worked as a domestic in white people's houses, and she told me that I was going to be my own maid and she'd pay me accordingly, like *she* got paid for housework. She started out by giving me

A GIFT OF LIFE

three dollars a week for doing my own laundry. Then I got a six-dollar-a-week raise for cooking dinner. If Mary came home early, we'd work together. We talked a lot and soon I didn't mind not having a sister. One day I called her Mama, and she hugged me and cried, and she *has* been "my mother" ever since.

So I had solved my problem at home. But I was still dissatisfied with the rest of my life. I wanted to *be somebody*, like the Reverend Jesse Jackson said later, and I knew I had to go somewhere else to accomplish it. I kept hoping and praying that my father's old wanderlust would return, and that he'd get a job somewhere far away and take Mary and me with him. Then, one day when I was fourteen, my prayers were answered. Daddy came in and said there was a job opening in a catering service up North. We were all going to move. I asked, "Whereabouts up North?"

"Lima, Ohio," he said.

3

In the patois of Hollywood, Sue Lovelace and Willie Coleman "met cute." This is the movie-industry expression for beginning a male-female relationship on-screen by having Marsha Mason, say, inadvertently lease the same apartment as Richard Dreyfuss. Or James Caan so pesters Marsha Mason on the telephone that she finally agrees to see him in person. In the old days, Doris Day "met cute" with nearly all her leading men.

It happens occasionally in the real world, too.

In Lima, Ohio, for instance.

Lima is a small, bustling city of some 50,000 people. It sits on the fertile plains and pretty wooded hills of west central Ohio, about halfway between Toledo and Dayton. It is a market town, a college town, a diverse manufacturing center, and the switchover point of a half dozen interstate railroad lines that crisscross its streets. More than a hundred years ago, Lima served as a switchover point for a different kind of interstate system, the Underground Railway, the route runaway slaves used to escape to the North.

Many blacks remained in Lima, to be joined by the second wave of immigration spawned by jobs made available in the reindustrialization of the area during and after World War II. The blacks still cluster in the southern end of town, in a pocket formed by the Norfolk & Western Railroad tracks and Interstate Highway 75.

Sue Lovelace lived there with her parents; Willie Coleman lived there with his parents; but it seemed highly unlikely they'd ever meet—cute or otherwise. Sue was sixteen and a student at Shawnee Junior High School, one of the prettiest and brightest girls in her ninth-grade class. Willie, at nineteen, was a high-school dropout, concerned only with advancing himself economically. Sue was a Methodist, Willie a Baptist. Sue was light-skinned, Willie dark-skinned. These were serious differences in a black community still bound by the traditions of the Old South, from which they had so recently departed.

And yet, it happened.

Willie

I didn't have anybody to guide me in those days.

There was nobody to tell me it was the most important thing to have an education to get ahead. So I had left school and was just trying to make as much money as I could wherever I could. Sometimes I had six jobs at a time. My main job was driving a truck for the Home Laundry and Dry Cleaning Service on Main Street, but I'd wash windows, clip hedges, do anything that came along. Still, I felt I must have been lacking because I liked to hang around with the high-school kids whenever I could.

On Halloween night in 1959 I went with a friend to a party in the neighborhood, and there was this pretty little girl who was at Shawnee Junior High with my sister. The young lady was introduced to me by her first name, Edmonia, not her middle name, Sue. "Ammonia?" I said, and she gave me a look that could kill. I kept trying to talk to her at the party, but I could see she cared as much for me as she cared for the water running in the creek.

Still, I followed her home and finally she turned and said, "Why don't you get lost?" I said, "Look, lady, I don't know where you come from, I don't care whether you like it or not, but one day you're going to be my wife." She went up the stairs to the porch of her house and slammed the door in my face.

A few days later, I was at work at Home Laundry when my boss, a feller named Bill Glover, who was later mayor of Lima, came up to me and asked if I wanted to make a couple of extra bucks. I said sure, and he told me to load a waxing machine and buffer in the truck and take them to his house to do the floors in his basement family room. His wife was going to have a big party there that weekend.

So I went to the Glover house and started working on the floor. The lady doing the housework there was Mary Lovelace. She watched me for a while and then she said, "I never seen a young feller work so hard. You seem smart, too. Are you going with anybody?" I said no. She said, "Do you know my daughter?" I said, "No, I don't know your daughter." She said, "Why don't you come over to the house next Sunday?"

So I went over to the Lovelace house on Sunday morning, and Sue and I were just sitting there glaring at each other, when Mary came in from church. I said, "Hello, Mary." Sue was so surprised I thought she was going to explode.

"Mary?" she yelled. "How come you calling her Mary? Do you two know each other?"

"Sure I do," said Mary, "and I'm the one who invited him over. He's the smartest, hardest-working young feller I've ever met in my life."

I guess that stamp of approval must have meant something to Sue because at least she tolerated me while I was there.

Mary Lovelace says, "It was an off-again, on-again romance for the next three years—mostly off-again. But I really did like that young feller. When he worked for a confectioner, the house was like a candy box; when he did odd jobs for a florist, the house was full of flowers. But Sue would date him for a while and then she wouldn't see him for months. Willie always came back, though."

Sue

Not much happened with Willie and me in the beginning because I really wasn't interested in him. I had a lot of other things on my mind. Most important of all to me was my education. I looked around me and saw that all these people who had come up from the South were doing the most menial jobs. The men were doing hard labor on construction sites or they were janitors or custodians, or, if they were like my father and Willie, they were picking up and delivering things. Most of the women, like Mary and Willie's mother, Luretha, were domestic workers. I knew that I had to study hard so that I could somehow break out of the housekeeping category. It's funny, but even in the big factories further north, where a lot of my father's relatives worked, that's what their departments were always called: Housekeeping. That meant that they hauled and cleaned and fetched and scrubbed.

I talked about this a lot with my mother, who was equally aware of it. She went to school at night to take a Licensed Practical Nurse course. She finished the course but couldn't pass the State Board exams. In the meantime, though, I listened to her talk about her classes and I pored through her books, and I was fascinated. I began to think this might be *my* way out of the "Housekeeping Trap": first, L.P.N. after I got out of high school, then, with more study, R.N.—Registered Nurse.

A GIFT OF LIFE

I dated Willie on and off through my three years at Lima High, along with some other boys. Gradually I came to like him quite a bit. He was opinionated and he argued a lot but he was also very sweet and considerate.

In my senior year in high school, however, something happened that made everything else seem unimportant. My father lost his job at the catering company, and because he was now in his fifties, he couldn't even get any of the construction work which was all that was available in Lima. I heard Dad put in a long distance phone call to his brother, my Uncle Eugene, who had taken Dad's job at the Abbott Laboratories when Dad had left Abbott several years before. Then Uncle Eugene came down to Lima to see us. He told Dad that Abbott was willing to take him back so that he could put in a few more years and earn a full Abbott pension.

We packed up and left immediately, even though I had only a few months to go to graduation. I was upset about that, but then I learned that if I just finished out the term at North Chicago High School, *they* would award me my diploma. And I really got excited when they told me that after graduation, I could take a Licensed Practical Nurse course at Waukegan High School, in conjunction with the adjacent Victory Memorial Hospital.

In the midst of my excitement, I did experience a little twinge of regret at never seeing Willie again, but I figured that was Fate. What I *didn't* figure on was Willie.

Willie

When Sue left Lima with her family in January 1962, I knew for sure that I was crazy about her. I had done everything in the world to make her jealous so she would want me. I had even got engaged to three other girls in succession, but I guess even that hadn't worked. Now I knew that all I could do was follow her, but I didn't want to let down my boss, Bill Glover at Home Laundry, who had been very nice to me, so I waited until my vacation time. Then I told him I was going up to Chicago and that I might or might not be back.

I got in my car and drove the nearly four hundred miles. I had never driven much outside of Lima and I was scared about going to the big city; but one thing about me, you just point me in the right direction and with God's help I get there. I went directly to my brother's house on Chicago's West Side. He couldn't understand how I managed to find his place without any directions.

For a few days I stayed with my brother until I could get up the nerve to phone Sue. When she sounded like she was glad to hear from me, I got real excited. She said she was lonely and missed me. She asked me where I was and when I told her Chicago, she said, "Oh, my." Then she asked me when I could come to see her. I said, "Right away," and I took off to North Chicago, which was forty miles away, like I had been making the trip all my life. I was nervous going up there because at that time Sue's father still hadn't come to reality about me. They didn't like dark complected people, no more than my family liked Sue at first because she was light-complected. Only Mary was on my side.

Anyway, I got to the Lovelace house at about eleven that night and I stayed there talking to Sue, nice and proper, until about two in the morning. I asked her to marry me and she said, Yes, yes, but that we couldn't make the engagement final until I decided to stay there and not go back to Lima.

On my way home to my brother's that night, I noticed a house in Waukegan with a sign in the window, "Room for Rent." I went to see the lady the next day and she told me she didn't rent to young, single men. I said, "I'm a churchgoer, I don't drink, I don't smoke, I'm not on the prowl." The landlady gave me a long look and said, "OK, you can have the room." Then I went to the Waukegan Post Office to send a money order to my mother and a man came by in a pickup truck and asked me if I wanted a three-month job doing construction work on Interstate 94, to start the next morning.

I said sure; then I hurried back to see Miss Lovelace. I told her I had a place to live and a job. Sue said, "Well, I guess you're permanent here now, so let's make it final that we're going to get married—in November."

I went to work on the highway pushing heavy wheelbarrows of cement, and Sue's mother immediately began making plans for a big church wedding. One night in November, Sue said to me,

"Do you think it's right for the folks to be spending all this money when they haven't got it?"

"I sure don't," I said. I called a friend of mine, name of L. C. Kraft, and I asked him if he'd go to the courthouse with us the next day, and also if he'd lend me fifteen dollars for the marriage license since I didn't get paid until Friday.

So nearly three years to the day when I first told Sue she was going to marry me, Miss Lovelace finally became Mrs. W. G. Coleman with L. C. Kraft and the court clerk as witnesses.

4

Gary Wayne Coleman did not come into the world until February 8, 1968, nearly six years after Sue and Willie were married.

The reasons for the delay were numerous.

First and foremost was the matter of economics. As Willie put it, "We just couldn't *afford* to start a family. Our struggle didn't really begin with Gary. For the first five years of our marriage, things were so bad in terms of money that we didn't know if we were going or coming."

Here were two young people, eighteen and twenty-two years old, in a more-or-less alien land, with practically no financial resources. The minimum wage then was $1.75 an hour and that's exactly what Willie was making on the construction job, or seventy dollars a week less deductions. Sue desperately wanted to fulfill her ambition of going to nursing school. But if she had, her only income would have been a "stipend" of fifty cents a day. So she had to put her dreams on the back burner for a while.

It was something of a miracle that they made it at all, but with an inner drive bordering on the ferocious—a trait later inherited by their son—they launched their own personal war on poverty. It was touch and go for quite a long time. Poverty nearly won.

The young couple moved in with Sue's parents. With his previous experience as a laundry driver in Lima, Willie talked his way into a job as laundry supervisor at Lake Forest Hospital. Supervisor or no, he was still taking home less than a hundred dollars a week and he had to haul huge heavy bundles of wet sheets and towels out of washing machines. Sue got work wherever she could, work like being a dietetic aide in the kitchen at the Veterans Hospital.

Determinedly independent, they moved out of the Lovelace house just as soon as they could. Although their combined incomes barely covered the rent, they got their own one-bedroom apartment when the first vacancy came up in the Marian Jones Housing Project near the Great Lakes Naval Training Station in North Chicago. The project was largely the home of Navy enlisted men and their families, but there was also a section for senior citizens. Willie and Sue were assigned to the seniors' section and the old folks were extraordinarily kind to the struggling young couple.

In 1964, the struggle became so intense that Willie collapsed while hauling a load of wet laundry. He was rushed, unconscious, to the emergency room and then into surgery. A diagnosis of acute appendicitis turned out to be a bleeding peptic ulcer, from which he had already hemorrhaged three and a half pints of blood. The recovery process took nine weeks, nine long weeks when he had no income at all—a factor that hardly helped the healing of a stress-induced ulcer.

When he recovered, Willie went back to work in his hospital laundry. By now, he and Sue were heavily in debt and had barely enough money to put soup or hot dogs or hamburger on the table.

But just when things seemed gloomiest, there came a series of fortuitous events, culminating in the birth of Gary.

Sue

One thing everyone should know about my husband: he's his own man, a strong man, a proud man. He could have made it easier on himself by walking into the employment office at the Abbott Laboratories and saying he was married to a Lovelace. Seven Lovelaces were already working there in the housekeeping department, including my father, and they all had excellent records. But Willie didn't want to trade on the Lovelace name, and he didn't want to be locked into a job in Housekeeping, mopping floors forever. He used to say, "We don't owe anybody anything—except for the good Lord—for keeping us going."

Then one day he had a scrape in the laundry room. Another supervisor, a black man who was actually a distant cousin of his, called him "nigger." Willie grabbed the man by the collar and slammed him against a wall. Then he walked into the hospital administrator's office and resigned. He doesn't know what made him do it, but at that moment he knew he had to get in his car and drive to the Abbott Laboratories a few miles away.

He went to the personnel office and asked for a job, using the Lovelace name. A man named Bob Lee came to interview Willie and must have liked what he heard. He asked him if he was interested in advancing himself by going back to school and getting his high school diploma. Willie said yes and Mr. Lee said, "OK, but first you'll have to push a broom for a little while." So for three months Willie pushed a broom, but at least he was making more money than he had gotten at the hospital laundry.

Three months to the day, Willie went back to Lee. "I can't wait until I get my diploma," he said. "I need the money now so I can start a family." The big break came a few days later when Dr. Eugene Woroch, head of the research lab, called Willie in. Dr. Woroch is a wonderful man who has been Willie's mentor. He said to Willie, "I like what I hear about you, young man. How would you feel about getting out of Housekeeping once and for all and taking a job as receiving clerk here in the lab? You'll have to keep track of all the chemicals in the stock room and get them to the scientists when they need them. But you *will* have to go back to school at the same time."

Willie said, "I'm ready to do whatever it takes to move up the ladder."

So Willie got the new job, at a lot more money, and he did very well. He was the only black person in the department, but his warm, outgoing personality made him immediately popular. He was the Santa Claus at the Christmas party, and he played golf with the men. He did, however, hesitate about going back to school. Dr. Woroch prodded him, Dr. Woroch's secretary, Judy Fritz, prodded him, a lady chemist named Anne Von Esch prodded him. I guess he was shy and scared about sitting in a classroom and taking tests after all those years.

The probability is that the principal prodding came from Sue herself, not by words but by example.

Sue finally was financially able to go to nursing school. The one year course took place in the nurses' quarters at Victory Memorial Hospital, even though it was administered by Waukegan High School. Sue learned basic patient care, dressing changes, and so on. Her practical work was done in the hospital itself on the orthopedics floor. With later amendments to the law regarding Licensed Practical Nurses in Illinois, they were permitted to dispense medications to patients, so that there also were courses in pharmacology and related subjects.

In 1966, when she graduated, Sue was hired by the hospital and went on regular duty on the orthopedics and surgical floors. She was respected, a paraprofessional, and determined to go even further, into the Registered Nurse course at Lake County Community

College. She was the first of the Lovelaces to break the old bonds.

Willie Coleman was prodded to the point where he once considered becoming a male nurse himself.

Then the prodding came from a different direction.

A child was on the way.

Sue

I never thought it would happen. I was still governed by the Old South thinking, and the legend was that the women in our family were all sort of infertile. My dad had two sisters and neither of them had children. My mom also had two sisters and neither of *them* had children. I had two first cousins on my father's side, a year or two older than I was, and they were both childless, too.

I didn't go to a doctor, even though I was working in the hospital, because my cousin, the eldest of the three of us, had gone through all kinds of medical workups. They had told her there really was nothing wrong, yet she couldn't get pregnant. I was kind of discouraged and I guess I believed the old wives' tales that it was a genetic thing—that being barren ran in our line.

So much for old wives' tales. In 1964, the sister of my cousin who had had the fertility workups suddenly got pregnant. Then, almost simultaneously, my other cousin and I also conceived.

All three of us, of course, worried constantly about miscarrying, but we all had perfectly normal pregnancies. I kept working in the hospital right into my eighth month. Then, with a fairly easy delivery, Gary was born there in the obstetrics ward of Victory Memorial. It was February 8, 1968. My son was nearly seven pounds and round and brown and beautiful. He was loud-mouthed and hungry.

There didn't seem to be anything in the world wrong with him.

Willie was beside himself with joy. After seeing his wife and new son at the hospital, he rushed back to Abbott. He could scarcely get into his office. The ladies of the department, led by Judy Fritz and Dr. Von Esch, had taken a collection, and Willie's cubicle was hung from floor to ceiling with dozens of diapers and other indispensable layette items.

5

When Gary was six months old, he rejected his bottle and refused to drink milk. This was the first sign that anything was wrong, but the warning went unheeded.

Before that, Willie and Sue found that they had an energetic and extremely bright son. At three months he was playing with beads strung over his crib, using both his hands and his feet. As he separated them in twos and threes, he almost seemed to be counting the beads. He played with his cuddly toys with great interest. He was extraordinarily attentive to the voices of his father and mother. Unusual sights and sounds fascinated him. Once, at Willie's parents' house in Lima, he stared at a window for a full ten minutes while a Norfolk and Western freight train roared by on the tracks outside. He insists he remembers the incident and that it marked the beginning of his all-consuming interest in trains which persists to this day. From the time he learned how to speak, he referred to Willie's mother, Luretha, as "Grandma who lives by the railroad."

Sue, in the meantime, had gone back to her nurse's job at Victory Memorial. She and Willie were good parents. They were still poor, though Dr. Woroch had assigned an Abbott loan officer to draw up a budget for them so they could get out of debt, and they couldn't afford a baby-sitter. Sue worked out a schedule to provide that either she or Willie would be at home with Gary at all times. She took the 11 P.M. to 7 A.M. shift at the hospital and Willie worked the 8 A.M. to 4 P.M. shift at Abbott. That gave them their evenings together, with Willie sleeping at night and Sue in the daytime. Gary was never alone.

As he grew out of infancy, Gary's height and weight were normal; his intelligence was decidedly above normal. Sue bought him picture books even before he was a toddler. She kept repeating the names of the animals in the books and soon he was pointing to the drawings and uttering his own approximation of the pronunciation of the names. He rarely made a mistake.

At five months, he was crawling furiously around the apartment; he was walking at ten months; he was talking at less than a year. His creative mischievousness was such that he learned to crawl onto a stool, turn on the tap in the bathroom sink and flood the apartment below.

With such unusual mental development and apparent good health, it is not surprising that Sue ignored Gary's first rejection of his milk bottle. He did drink milk sporadically for a while, but he obviously preferred fruit juices and just plain water in his bottle. As he approached his first birthday, his favorite drink was water.

Then one day he did an extraordinary thing.

Sue came home from work that morning, and, as she always did, she filled his bottle with milk and attempted to get him to drink it. Gary stared at the bottle for a moment. Then he leaned over from his high chair, lined up the nearby garbage pail, and scored a perfect slam-dunk with the bottle.

Sue

The most important advice I give to parents today is to listen to the child. He's worth listening to. He may know things *you* don't know. Back in those early days with Gary, I wasn't smart enough to follow that advice. He couldn't speak yet, but he was trying to communicate with me as best he could.

By tossing the bottle in the garbage pail, he was telling me that the white stuff in the bottle hurt him inside when he drank it. He was way ahead of me and I should have listened. I didn't find out until much later that the lactic acid in milk *does* irritate kidney tissue that isn't functioning properly. So I just kept giving him water, instead of milk, with his baby food; and I didn't even tell our pediatricians, Dr. Julius Wineberg and Dr. Barry Goldman. Around the hospital, I heard the nurses in Pediatrics talking about babies with milk allergies and I simply chalked it up to that.

There was no reason to think otherwise. Gary

kept growing and thriving and he was always what I call "bouncy playing"—in trouble all the time, poking his way into places where he wasn't supposed to be. We got older children's toys for him—building blocks and such—and they fascinated him. Dr. Goldman was very pleased with his mental and physical advancement at that age.

Only one thing bothered me. He was thirsty all the time and drank a lot of water. Remembering what I knew from the hospital, I worried that this might be a warning symptom of diabetes. But the doctors did a blood sugar during his regular checkup and there was nothing wrong. Aside from that, Gary would have occasional episodes of high fever and a little chest congestion—like all children do. I'd give him aspirin, maybe sponge him. The temperature would come down in a few hours and then he'd be fine.

So I was completely unprepared when he got really sick just before Christmas in 1969. He was twenty-two months old at the time. He had been playing outside in the snow with Willie and when he came in, we both could see that he was listless and not like himself. No bouncy playing. He also had a nasty sounding cough. We figured he just had caught a cold out there in the snow, but to be sure, I rushed to get the thermometer. His temperature was 104. I still wasn't worried because of those high temperatures he'd run before, but something told me to have Willie bring the car around so we could take Gary over to our pediatrician's office.

It was Dr. Wineberg this time. He examined Gary, listening to his chest with his stethoscope. The temperature was still up around 104. Dr.

Wineberg said, "It might be a slight case of pneumonia, and it might be something else. Let's get him over to the hospital right away."

We went over to Victory Memorial, and the way you do in times like that, I had the craziest thought: I was going on duty five hours early that day. Gary was admitted and they immediately took chest X-rays. Everything pointed to pneumonia because he had the chest congestion and the runny nose and the difficult breathing, and all.

It was now eight o'clock and Gary was resting comfortably, so I told Willie to go home and get some sleep because he had to go to work early the next morning. I had only three hours before my duty started, so I decided to stay on. I was worried, because in spite of the first tentative diagnosis of mild pneumonia, they kept doing workups on Gary.

Dr. Wineberg found that Gary was dehydrated and he ordered fluids to be given intravenously. The doctor seemed puzzled. Then he asked me if I had been giving Gary a lot of aspirin to bring the fever down. I told him, "No more than five grains," but he ordered a salicylate level. It turned out negative. Dr. Wineberg said, "OK, let's check for sickle-cell anemia." I knew they did that with all black children and that some of the symptoms of sickle cell are difficult breathing and high temperature. But again the tests were negative.

They let Gary rest for a while and Dr. Wineberg left, and at eleven P.M. I went upstairs to report for duty on my orthopedics floor. As soon as I could, I popped down to see Gary again. This time, Dr. Wineberg's associate, Dr. Goldman,

A GIFT OF LIFE

was there, sitting at Gary's bedside and staring at him. Dr. Goldman kept asking me if Gary had been sick prior to this, what symptoms? I told him about the few chest colds and the high fevers, which disappeared with aspirin and sponging. He nodded and said, "Well, there's nothing to do but make a complete series of blood chemistries. This child is too sick for what I can see physically."

The rest of the night was a nightmare for me. I worked my floor and I kept running down to Pediatrics and to the lab where they were doing the blood chemistries. I knew enough about the electrolyte tests the technicians were doing, and from what they told me—that everything was haywire, out of kilter. They were trying to stabilize him by changing the intravenous fluids, but nothing seemed to work. Gary's white blood count was way up, which meant that his body was trying to fight off a very serious infection somewhere. They began to pinpoint the "somewhere" when they found red blood cells in the urine and high levels of creatinine in the blood.

By now it was morning and Willie was there again. The doctors said they were bringing in a distinguished urologist, Dr. Francis Richardson. They asked us to sign release forms for Dr. Richardson to do a cystoscopy—looking up into the bladder with a special instrument—and also a very complicated kind of X-rays of the kidneys. For the first time, I panicked. I knew what that might mean.

Dr. Richardson came in at about eleven A.M. He was a very dignified older man who I had seen around the hospital. He did the cystoscopy and took the X-rays, which required Gary to drink a solution that would make the soft tissues of the kidneys and the urinary tract visible on the X-ray. It took hours and Gary, poor sick child, faded in and out of sleep. They kept hauling him hither and yon. He looked up at me from time to time, kind of pleading, but he never once cried. Whenever he did that, I had a hard time keeping myself together.

Finally, Dr. Richardson called me into the X-ray room. He showed me X-rays of a normal child's kidneys, with the ureter tubes leading straight down from the kidneys to the bladder, where harmful substances removed by the kidneys are flushed out of the body as urine. Then he showed me Gary's X-rays. The tubes were all twisted up like spaghetti.

Dr. Richardson explained that some sort of blockage was causing fluids to back up the tubes and into the kidneys. Poisons were leaking out of the kidneys into the body cavity and causing uremia. The general infection already had involved the lungs, which is why Gary was showing pneumonia symptoms. Dr. Richardson was trying to spare me by not telling me any more, but I knew that if uremia spreads through the system and isn't checked, it can be fatal. After all those hours I finally broke down and cried when I realized that Gary's little tummy was already swollen up all out of proportion. I remembered those pictures of babies with distended bellies dying in the famine areas of Africa.

But I got control of myself and I said, "OK, Doctor. What do we do now?"

Dr. Richardson said, "We transfer him im-

A GIFT OF LIFE

mediately to Children's Memorial Hospital in Chicago for surgery."

By now, Willie had come in. He said, "Then it's in God's hands."

Dr. Richardson said, "Yes, and also in the hands of the finest team of young pediatric urologists in this area."

So Gary and Sue and Willie made the first of their many fifty-mile trips to Children's Memorial.

Actually, once they resigned themselves to the fact of the surgery, Sue and Willie were not too anxious about it. The doctors at Victory Memorial had gone out of their way to allay their fears. The uremia could be controlled and the obstruction causing the backup might not be a serious surgical problem. Probably to avoid frightening the young parents—Sue then was twenty-six and Willie thirty—they allowed them to drive Gary to Chicago themselves, rather than ordering an ambulance. Willie was mainly concerned about finding his way in the Big City, and the doctors gave him precise directions.

With Willie's uncanny sense of direction, the trip was uneventful. Gary, long since toilet-trained, now was diapered again and catheterized. He spent most of the journey dozing in his mother's arms. When they arrived at the hospital, Sue became alarmed again as, immediately after Gary's admission, the nurses seemed to be preparing the child for surgery that evening, and it was already late in the afternoon. Maybe it really *was* terribly serious. The head of the surgical team came in. His name was Dr. Barry Belman, and like most of the others Sue had seen, he was young, still in his thirties. He told her, "We're not operating tonight. We'll do the surgery at seven tomorrow morning." She felt reassured—but not much.

Willie went home and a cot was brought into Gary's room so Sue could spend the night with him. It was her first time in a hospital not her own, in which she did not know nurses and technicians to keep her apprised of what was going on and she felt disoriented as well as frightened. Several times during the night, however, young Toni Greenslade came in and Sue struck up a tentative nurse-to-nurse rapport with her. Ms. Greenslade was to be Gary's nurse for many years to come. Sue liked her and respected her at first sight, and was finally able to relax enough to get some sleep.

At 6:30 A.M., Willie returned from Zion and a half hour later, Gary was wheeled away to the operating room.

Sue

I had no idea of what they were doing to Gary, but when Toni Greenslade told me he'd be out of surgery and in the recovery room in about four hours, I didn't worry too much. Four or five hours in surgery was nothing really out of the ordinary at that time.

So even though we had been on an emotional roller coaster ever since Gary got sick, Willie and I were not quite prepared for what Dr. Belman had to say when he came out to talk to us at about noon. He began by reassuring us that Gary was fine as far as the immediate problem was concerned. The uremic poisoning had been drained and now was being managed.

Then came the bad news.

"When we went in, we found that Gary's right kidney was not functioning," Dr. Belman said. "It was atrophied and probably had been that way at birth. Because of the backup of urine, the left kidney is already damaged and only working at about forty percent capacity. That's all right. Even a forty percent single kidney can carry the load for the entire body.

"But," he added, "cells have been damaged and some of them don't regenerate themselves, so there's a very strong possibility that the left kidney, too, will atrophy. We're sure that Gary will need a transplant. But we want to wait until he's older, more developed and stronger. In the meantime, we've disconnected the ureter tubes that run from the kidney to the bladder and they now run from the kidney to surgical openings we've made in his sides. He'll no longer urinate with his penis. The urine will drain through the new openings. No pouch yet. He's too young. You'll just have to keep him diapered all the time, around his entire torso."

We were still trying to take all this in when Dr. Belman said, "In a way, your Gary is lucky."

Willie said, "*Lucky?* How so?"

"If he hadn't come down with that pneumonia, and if he hadn't been hospitalized," Dr. Belman explained, "the far more serious kidney problem might not even have been diagnosed until it was too late."

"And when would be too late?" Willie asked.

"About a month from now," Dr. Belman said.

6

The circumstantial discovery of Gary's congenital and near-fatal kidney problem was not unusual back in 1969. Such chance diagnosis still occurs today, even with the enormous strides that have been made in the last decade in the field of pediatric nephrology, as it is called, *nephros* being the Greek word for kidney.

Dr. Ira Greifer of the Albert Einstein Medical Center in New York is considered by many to be the dean of the relatively new medical science of pediatric nephrology. Dr. Greifer explains that before a baby is born, it excretes through its mother's kidneys. Thus, even if the newborn infant has congenital kidney malfunction, it has been able to develop normally in the uterus and can appear to be symptom-free at birth.

Dr. Greifer says, "Sometimes there's a distended

stomach at birth. That's the one good clue. But remember that you need only one partially operating kidney for seemingly normal function. So if the baby urinates well, an atrophied second kidney, or another serious problem like Gary Coleman had—obstructive disease of the tubular system—can go undetected for years. Later, there are other clues which bring the kidney malfunction to our attention: lack of growth, behavioral disorders, maybe a problem with infection. It was fortunate, indeed, that Gary had excellent physicians who spotted the unusual aspects of that lung infection when the child was still less than two years old. Especially back in those early days when we knew so much less than we do now. The very first transplants on children had been done only two years before, in 1967."

Dr. Greifer, among his other duties and honors, is medical director of the National Kidney Foundation, which is to kidney disease what the American Cancer Society is to cancer and what the American Heart Association is to heart ailments. Based in New York City at 2 Park Avenue, the National Kidney Foundation is mainly privately funded and monitors research throughout the United States. It is the main conduit for dispensing information about kidney disease to the public and to doctors.

As an indication of how little was known about the kidney until recently, the Foundation had its tentative beginnings in 1954 and was only incorporated in 1964.

Long after great advances were made in the management of other serious illnesses, kidney disease remained the most largely unexplored and unconquered invader of the human body. In the first quarter of the twentieth-century, more people died of kidney malfunction (82.9 people in every 100,000) than cancer (77.3 per 100,000).

It is only in the last fifty years that the kidney itself has become fairly well understood by science.

It is a fascinating organ.

Normally, each of us has two kidneys located on either side of the spine at the lowest level of the rib cage. An adult kidney weighs about a quarter of a pound and is fist-sized, in the shape of the familiar kidney bean. Each kidney contains about a million tiny units called nephrons. The nephrons comprise a filtering system so remarkable that scientists still shake their heads at the wonder of it all.

The blood enters the kidneys directly from the aorta, the main artery that pumps blood from the heart. As the blood passes through the million nephrons in each kidney, a microscopic tuft, the glomerulus, in every nephron removes wastes and poisons and passes the remainder of the blood, about 99 percent, into what is called a tubule. The tubule completes the blood-cleaning process. All the essential life-sustaining elements in the blood are then returned to the body through a major vein, the vena cava. The wastes and poisons become urine, which passes down the ureter tube to the bladder from which it is excreted.

In every 24 hours, some 200 quarts of blood are filtered this way, with 198 quarts returning to the bloodstream and two quarts of waste exiting the body as urine. The National Kidney Foundation compares the process to the space-ship apparatus that automatically controls temperature, humidity and oxygen so that the internal environment within

A GIFT OF LIFE

the space ship can support life. If the instruments were to fail to function, the environment inside the ship would go bad, and life within it would cease.

The great physiologist, Dr. Homer W. Smith, once put it another way, "Bones can break, muscles can atrophy, glands can loaf, even the brain can go to sleep without immediate danger to survival. But should the kidneys fail, neither bones, muscles, glands nor brain could carry on."

So much for the absolute essentiality of the kidney. But what makes it go wrong?

There are literally dozens of diseases of the kidney, most of them with jaw-breaking names. There is pyelonephritis, an infectious inflammation of the tissue of the kidneys; there is nephrosis, in which there is an unexplained leakage from the glomerulus; there is glomerulonephritis, caused by a streptococcus infection. There is a birth defect called polycystic kidneys, in which the kidney tissue is filled with cysts, small holes and fluid-filled cavities.

There are abscesses of the kidney, tuberculosis of the kidney, tumors of the kidney. There are diseases of the kidney associated with high blood pressure, diabetes, accidents, prolonged exposure to such substances as mercury and the cleaning fluid, carbon tetrachloride. What Gary had is known technically as congenital obstructive uropathy leading to hydronephrosis. In his case the exact cause of the obstruction was not known until later.

In all, according to the latest government statistics, some 13,000,000 Americans are under treatment for one or the other of this large collection of multi-syllabic kidney diseases, and about 50,000 die each year. It is estimated that at least 3,300,000 Americans are walking around with undetected, undiagnosed diseases of the kidney and many of them will die if they do not receive medical help. Until the onset of the great medical advances in fairly recent years, the statistics were much worse.

The first major breakthrough came in 1944, in, of all places, Nazi-occupied Holland. Working under the worst possible circumstances, a Dutch doctor named Willem Kolff constructed a crude dialysis machine, first using a sausage casing and later cellophane as a membrane to filter the poisons out of the blood, much as a natural kidney does. Dr. Kolff was the first to accomplish this feat with a human patient—a man in the terminal stages of uremia.

After World War II, Dr. Kolff came to the United States and turned his blueprints over to a medical team at Peter Bent Brigham Hospital in Boston. The team, headed by Dr. John P. Merrill, improved the apparatus to such an extent that by 1950, a patient could be dialyzed five or six times and kept alive over a period of months. A dialysis machine is about the size of an electric clothes washer. It pumps the blood out of an artery, usually in the patient's arm, "washes" it through a series of membranes, and then returns it to a vein, also usually in the patient's arm.

These advances with dialysis made it possible to keep a kidney patient alive long enough to make transplantation possible. The first successful kidney transplant in history took place on December 23, 1954, at Peter Bent Brigham. Dr. Joseph E. Murray performed the actual surgery, but again, the remarkable pioneer, Dr. Merrill, was a key member of the team. The patient, still alive today, was a woman who received a kidney from an identical twin. Dr.

A GIFT OF LIFE

Merrill was honored by the National Kidney Foundation in 1979, the twenty-fifth anniversary of the trailblazing event.

The second big breakthrough in transplantation occurred in 1962 when the first successful transplant was done with a kidney from a non-related donor. Such "foreign" tissue invariably is rejected by the defense mechanisms in the body—as witness the failure thus far of most *heart* transplants—but it was learned that rejection of the kidney could be prevented by giving the patient so-called immunosuppressive drugs, usually steroids which are synthetic forms of cortisone. So most donated kidneys soon came from otherwise healthy people who died in auto accidents or from other causes that did not affect the kidney itself. By law, the donation must be made by the closest relative of the deceased.

Until 1973, when Gary Coleman's transplant operation took place, nephrology progressed at a breakneck pace, but the progress was accompanied by tragedy and heartbreak. The cost of both transplantation and dialysis was astronomical. Only the very rich could afford either. Not only that, but the donors were few and so were the expensive dialysis machines. Dr. Ira Greifer remembers when there were only one or two machines in a hospital and a "death committee" of doctors was set up to determine who would go on the machine and live, and who would not go on the machine and die.

But then, in 1973, Congress passed one of the most important health measures it has ever enacted. The bill, known simply as H.R. 1, funded billions of dollars for dialysis machines and kidney transplantation operations. Banks of dialysis machines were provided to all hospitals that needed them. Besides, all costs—both for dialysis and transplantation—would be paid out of Medicare funds in the Social Security system, no matter how young or old the patient happened to be.

As a result, 61,000 Americans who otherwise would be dead are healthy today, either with kidney transplants or through the life giving procedures of now-totally-accessible dialysis. Although transplants still are only about 40 percent successful in staving off rejection for the critical period of the first two years, a millennium of sorts arrived with H.R. 1 in 1973.

Four years earlier, when Gary Coleman underwent his first surgical procedure at Children's Memorial Hospital in Chicago, Willie and Sue were totally unaware of the coming millennium. They also were unaware of the general opinion among nephrologists at the time that transplantation was unsuitable for children. Dr. Greifer says, "It was thought that children were too susceptible to other diseases to risk breaking down their body's defense system with the immunosuppressive drugs necessary to prevent the rejection of the transplanted kidney."

All that Willie and Sue knew and cared about was that their child was alive, even though he could urinate only through those strange surgical openings in his sides.

7

When Gary came home from the hospital that first time, an immediate problem faced Sue. Since his urine now was draining freely and constantly from the openings (which were constructed of intestinal tissue "like the turned-back end of a hose," as she puts it), Gary needed dozens of diapers a day. Sue worked out a system of stringing several diapers together with safety pins and wrapping them around Gary's middle. At that point though, the Colemans were too poor to buy a washing machine for the laundering of so many diapers every day. With Willie working days and Sue putting in her full eight hours at the hospital every night, it was both exhausting and impractical for either of them to sit around a commercial laundromat waiting for the vast bundle of diapers to be washed and dried.

There was only one solution: to move back into Sue's parents' home, where there was a washer and dryer, a small apartment upstairs and some much-needed nursing help from Mary.

Sue

My mother and father always were there to take over when I was at work or asleep, but the main nursing burden fell to me, of course. In a way, it was therapy for me, and over the years, I'm sure it helped me keep my sanity. I said to myself, over and over again, "I'm the nurse on this case and Gary is my patient." So when things got tough for me emotionally as Gary's mother, I'd lose myself in the duties I had to perform as Gary's nurse.

I'd make sure he followed his schedule of medication, just as I did with any other patient in the hospital. Also, every morning, I'd bathe him in the tub, wash him good with soap, and then I'd apply an antiseptic cream to the surgical openings to keep them free of bacteria. Then, at least a couple of times a day, I'd coat his skin all around the area with Vaseline, to keep the urine from irritating him as it dripped out into the diapers. In addition to all this, the diapers had to be changed and washed.

I worked very closely with the doctors, which made it possible for us to keep Gary at home more, instead of his having to stay in the hospital under nursing supervision for weeks on end. As it was, Willie and I only had to drive Gary to Children's Memorial once every three weeks. After a while, we were able to cut down the hospital visits to once a month.

At first, Gary was taken care of by Dr. Belman, who had done the surgery, but then Dr. Peter Lewy, another fine young doctor in the nephrology team, became Gary's regular pediatric nephrologist and kept tabs on the function of Gary's one remaining kidney. Dr. Lewy would do dozens of tests every time we came to the hospital. Then he'd let Gary go home with us. I noticed that he'd keep other children, with the same condition, in the hospital.

"I felt perfectly safe with Gary in Sue's care," Dr. Lewy told me. "She's a remarkable, skilled, dedicated woman. Also very courageous—the classic American heroine. I know of other children who didn't make it but who might have if they'd had mothers like Sue."

With Sue and Willie's care, Gary developed normally, and except for the bulky layers of diapers around his waist that made him look like an overstuffed teddy bear, he was like any other two-year-old. Gary has remarkable though understandably spotty memory of the events of his early childhood. With his extraordinary brightness, one does tend to forget that he is, after all, still a child, and he has child-oriented recollections.

Gary

I can remember my mom wrapping me up with diapers just like you wrap a bandage around a finger when you've cut it.

I remember when we lived in the Mary Ann Jones apartments when I was just a little baby and I only could say coo-coo and goo-goo all the time. Our apartment had a green door and the street was sort of like ricky-racky and it was all predominantly black. There were a lot of buildings, one-floor ones and two-floor ones. I used to lie in my crib and listen to the radio a lot, but I got Mom mad by getting out of my crib and crawling over to the window to watch all the people and listen to them talk.

We only had one bedroom and my crib was in it. Mom and Dad slept in the living room on a folding bed which we still have. I mustn't have been even a year old yet, but I remember one night when I couldn't sleep because of all the people talking outside. I had my own teddy bears, which I played with, and I had some wafer cookies, which are still my favorite. I played with the teddy bears and ate the cookies, but I still couldn't sleep because of the voices of the people outside the window. I still remember what they were saying, things like, "Hey, man," "Give me a card, man," and "Let's go around the block and have some fun."

So I climbed over the rail of the crib, and I got onto a chair and then down onto the floor. I

A GIFT OF LIFE

crawled over to the door, which was not locked but on the latch, and I wanted to open the door so I could get in bed with Mom and Dad. But I was still about six inches too short to reach the door knob. So I bumped against the door, like a dumb baby, trying to jump up and grab the door knob and turn it. Finally I got the door open and went crawling through the house, crying. That's when Mom and Dad came to get me and put me in bed with them to shut me up.

The next thing I remember was going to live in Grandma and Grandpa's house in Waukegan. The house was box-type and had a brown door. We lived upstairs and all day long I was going down the stairs, to Grandma's and Grandpa's, and back up again. Once, they were making popcorn, and the popcorn was popping all over the floor, and I was eating the popcorn from the floor. Mom smacked me good for that. Another time, I put a paper bag over my head and was riding around in circles on my tricycle on the front walk, which had a crack in it. All of a sudden, I went crashing down the steps because I couldn't see with the bag over my head. I ended up with the tricycle on top of me and the empty bag on the ground. I wasn't hurt, but Mom smacked me good for that, too.

It was a nice house with a beautiful garden in the back that Grandpa kept planted. I used to ride a pedal-truck up and down the front walk while Dad washed his car on the lawn. I had lots of kids in the neighborhood to play with, mostly cousins and nephews. No, they *all* were cousins. I'm not old enough yet to have nephews.

I remember going to the hospital a lot with

Mom and Dad. That was fun, too. The nurses were nice, and they let me move my bed up and down with the electric controls, and they filled the whole bottom of my bed with toys. The doctors did a lot of things to me, but they didn't hurt me much. One day, Mom and Dad took me to the hospital and the doctors kept me there for a few days. They put me to sleep and when I woke up, I had a plastic pouch attached to my belly to pee in. It was as simple as that, and I didn't have to pee any more into those dumb diapers Mom used to wrap around my middle all the time.

This was Gary's second major surgery and it was neither as simple nor as much fun as he recalls it, which is understandable, since he was only three and a half years old at the time.

The year was 1971.

At Children's Memorial, Dr. Lewy had been carefully testing Gary's kidney function, and he didn't like what he saw. The remaining left kidney was slowly beginning to fail. The useless right kidney, with which Gary had been born, was just lying there and possibly impeding the over-all nephrotic process. Since it had been determined from the beginning that Gary would eventually require a transplant, it was necessary to find out, once and for all, the location of the congenital obstruction which had caused the damage to the kidneys in the first place. And, of course, the obstruction had to be removed before the future transplant could even be considered, or the new kidney would just go the way of the old—damaged and eventually atrophied by the backflow of urine, leading to the condition called hydronephrosis.

A GIFT OF LIFE

Dr. Lewy conferred with the surgeon, Dr. Belman, among others on the nephrology team. It was determined that this was an excellent time to do the pretransplant repair work. Gary was in otherwise good health; he had no uremia as he did at the time of the first operation. His body now was strong and much better developed to withstand a complicated triple operation. Surgery was scheduled for the very next time Gary came in for his checkup, but Sue and Willie were not told so as not to unduly alarm them.

What Dr. Belman did during this surgery was to first remove the atrophied right kidney, completely and permanently closing off the blood flow from the aorta on that side. Next came the all-important search for the obstruction in the urinary tract. Because Gary had had no further problems since the ureters were severed from the bladder and attached to the openings in his sides, it was obvious that the obstruction was either in the bladder or below it.

Below the bladder is the urethra, a canal through which urine drains out via the penis in males, and the urethral opening in the vulva in females. As Lewy and Belman suspected, there, indeed, was the obstruction—little flaps of tissue clogging the urethra. The flaps were congenital, meaning that Gary had been born with them. Science still has no explanation of how and why such an abnormality occasionally occurs.

The culprit having finally been identified, Belman and Lewy decided to leave the flaps for the time being. It would be much easier to clean them out later in a simpler nonsurgical procedure involving instruments inserted through the penis.

Finally, the doctors decided to improve the makeshift process whereby Gary's urine was draining into the diapers through the surgical openings in his sides. They closed up the openings and made a single new one in his lower abdomen. The ureter from the remaining left kidney was extended to the new opening with intestinal tissue, once again bypassing the still unusable bladder. A plastic pouch now could be attached to the new opening to catch the urine draining down through the ureter from the kidney. The pouch, in effect, was an outside bladder. It was removable and could be reattached to the skin surrounding the opening with a strong, medical mucilage. Normally, the pouch would not be removed except for cleaning. At the bottom of the pouch was a valve which Gary himself could unscrew and allow the urine to drain out, almost as if he were urinating normally.

Once again, it was a temporary measure but immensely more convenient.

And Gary, now nearly four, had seen the last of his diapers.

8

Although the major crisis still lay ahead, Gary could now assume the outward trappings of normality for a little boy. He could dress, play, run around, go sightseeing and visiting with his parents, just like any other youngster. Once he learned to use it, the pouch proved no more than a minor inconvenience. Sue attached it in the morning, making a snug seal with the adhesive, and then fastened the device in place with a belt. Gary insisted on doing all the emptying of the pouch, going to the bathroom and unscrewing the bottom valve whenever the bag began to bulge. In later years he complained that the pouch sometimes became so heavy with urine that it caused him to stoop over, "giving me a poor posture." Sue refutes this theory as being pure nonsense.

Gary

I guess Mom's right. I don't have bad posture, and even if I did, the pouch didn't have anything to do with it. Actually, that old pouch wasn't so bad. I just had to remember to empty it every two or three hours, because I never knew when it was full. It wasn't like a real bladder, which *tells* you when you've got to go to the bathroom.

Most of all, I didn't want the other kids to know about it and pick on me, so I tried to go to the toilet where no one else could see me. When I couldn't do that, I learned how to unzip my pants and just take out the bottom of the pouch so I could unscrew the valve and make it look like I was peeing with my penis.

Until I learned how to handle it, the worst time was at night. If the bag was full and I rolled over on it, the glue could tear loose from the skin around the opening in my belly, and, boy, there would be a real mess in the bed. But I never had an accident. I taught myself to sleep on my back, which I never did before. In the beginning, Mom or Dad would get up two or three times a night to take me to the bathroom to empty the pouch. But then I said, "You don't have to get up. You both work hard and need your sleep. I can handle it myself."

So I concentrated real hard and made like an alarm clock in my head, and sure enough, I would wake up every night at about two in the morning and go empty the pouch by myself.

A GIFT OF LIFE

• • •

Sue continued, as Gary's nurse, to keep the new abdominal opening clean and germ-free. She and Willie exulted in the fact that they now could take Gary anywhere and that—unless he was closely observed in the bathroom—no one could be aware that he was any different from any other little boy. For the first time since their son's initial uremia in 1969, some sort of normality could return to their lives, too, and even with the continuing gnawing dread of what still was to come, they could concentrate again on their own personal goals.

Willie, in particular. His quest for education and advancement had been delayed by the trauma of Gary's illness and the special care the child required when he was swathed in diapers. Now, the old yearnings and ambitions returned, intensified by something that happened at Children's Memorial while Gary was in the hospital for the second surgery. Fascinated with the fetching little boy, the doctors gave him the standard intelligence test for children of that age. When Willie and Sue asked for the results they were told, "His IQ is so high that it's better that you don't know."

Willie

I'd look at Gary every night when I got home from work, and I'd think about that intelligence test and where he could go in life, God willing, if I could provide for him right. Then I'd look at Sue. I had worked hard to put her through nursing school, and she had already advanced herself pretty far. I searched myself and I decided, what the heck, *I'm* going to be somebody, too. But first, there's so much knowledge to take in. I was scared. After all, I hadn't been to school in maybe fifteen years.

Sue became a driving force and so did Dr. Woroch and nearly everybody else at Abbott. Anne Von Esch, a chemist in the lab, especially got after me now. In her spare time she was active at the North Chicago Community High School, trying to get people like me to go there to study for the high school equivalency exam. It wasn't that I'd immediately get a promotion if I got the diploma. The main thing was that they'd respect me for doing it.

So I went to Anne Von Esch and she guided me in how to register at the night school. Man, it was tough. After all, I was thirty-two years old. But I stuck with it, and Sue and everybody at the plant kept cheering me on, and after three months the teacher told me I was ready to go to Springfield, the state capital, to take the exam.

I drove down to Springfield with six other people. I sat in this big room mostly with kids much younger than me. I wrote the answers to the questions and all the time I was thinking the funniest things, like maybe my doing this would be an inspiration to my younger brothers. But I only got a 74 and the clerk told me I needed two more points to pass. He said I could take the test again in seventy-two hours. So in seventy-two hours, I went down to Springfield again.

This time I got an 82. I called Sue and she cried, and when I got home she had a lot of people in the house for a party for me and my diploma.

This is really how my whole life came about in the way of changing.

In these days of multiple master's degrees and doctorates, a simple high school diploma might not seem like much. But it did to Eugene L. Woroch, Ph.D., M.A. M.S. M.B.A., then the head of the research facility and now director of an entire division of the multinational Abbott Laboratories, Inc.

Says Dr. Woroch, "More than anything else, much more than what he could have learned in three months in school, that diploma demonstrated to us that Willie had a lot of motivation and drive. Actually, by that time he didn't even need the diploma to advance in the company. He had already displayed the qualities of dedication, conscientiousness and responsibility. Also, he was so intelligent that we had Willie doing some reasonably sophisticated things. We entrusted him with the cataloguing and coding of new chemicals as they came in, for example, and we always knew that if a product had to be refrigerated, Willie would see that it was refrigerated instead of just being put on a shelf to spoil. So I think he basically wanted to earn our respect and show what he was capable of doing by getting the diploma. If so, he succeeded."

The company, on the other hand, succeeded in demonstrating that a huge corporation can be both benevolent and compassionate to a motivated, conscientious employee. Having first worked out arrangements with Willie's many creditors and devising a personal budget to help the Colemans escape from the worrisome trap of indebtedness, the Abbott Health Plan now paid Gary's overwhelming medical bills before the advent of H.R. 1. Also, it was an Abbott executive who, out of his own pocket, made it possible for the Colemans to buy their first house and escape the equally worrisome confines of the ghetto.

It was little Gary's winsomeness that helped in the escape, too.

Sue

My father had now put in enough years to earn his retirement pension at Abbott, and he and my mother wanted to go back to Lima, to a more rural atmosphere. Since they were going to sell the house in Waukegan, we began to look for another apartment for ourselves. I didn't need their wonderful daily help anymore, or even their washer and dryer.

So Willie and I went to a real estate broker. We found an apartment and actually had put a deposit on it, when the broker said, "Would you kids like to buy a house?" We said, "Of course we would, but we can't afford one." He said, "Well, let's not worry about that right now. I have the perfect house for you. It's not up for show yet, but I think it's just right for you and so is the price." He did some quick figuring and he mentioned a deposit which we could just about meet by cashing in all our savings bonds. He also said we'd have to come up with seven hundred dollars in closing costs.

I figured in my head that I had maybe two hundred and fifty dollars in my savings account and that Willie, paying off all our previous debts, was still taking home about $4.98 a week, but we said, "Yes, we're very interested." The broker said he'd call us as soon as the house was open to be seen.

We got in the car and drove right over to 31st Street in Zion to look at the house from the outside. We immediately fell in love with it. It was a small neat bungalow, painted yellow, with a big lawn in front and a huge yard in back. Willie said, "Oh, my, I could plant flowers and I could do this and I could do that."

Only one thing worried us. The neighborhood was all white. We didn't see a black face for blocks around.

Anyway, we went home and I had a dream that night, in which I could see the kitchen, small and practical, with knotty-pine paneling. When I woke up in the morning, I had to tell myself to stop hoping.

But a few days later, the real estate broker called and we drove over to see the house. It was owned by an elderly white couple, the Carl Millers, who were retired and wanted to go to Florida in their mobile home. Willie took one look at the kitchen and said, "Good Lord, it's just like you saw it in your dream."

It was Gary who swung it for us. He was a cute little four-year-old kid running around and enjoying himself, and the Millers couldn't take their eyes off him. They picked him up and bounced him around. He kept chattering away in that adult way of his, and they were enchanted. Mrs. Miller even took him next door to see her sister and she said, "Look what we have here." Then she came back and said, "If you really want the house, we won't show it to anyone else."

We said we did want the house more than anything in our whole lives. We were so excited we couldn't think of anything else for weeks. We managed to get the deposit together and a bank came up with the mortgage. But then the whole dream seemed about to fall apart.

There was no way we were going to be able to come up with that seven hundred dollars for the closing costs.

Willie

I was at work and so upset that I could hardly do anything. It kept troubling me in my mind that we were so close to getting that house and we were going to blow it because of those closing costs. I was so far extended that I couldn't borrow that seven hundred dollars nowhere.

The phone rang in my little office and it was Dr.

A GIFT OF LIFE

Warren Close. He was the divisional manager, the highest boss in my part of the company. Dr. Close told me to come up to see him. I went to his office, wondering if I had done something wrong.

The first thing he said was, "I understand that you and Sue have found a house that you really want." I nodded, wondering how such a high ranking man even knew about it. He said, "How much money do you need for the closing costs?" I told him it was seven hundred dollars and that there ain't nowhere on this green earth that I could get seven hundred dollars.

He said, "Well, Coleman, let me let you in on a little secret. I'm pretty well-to-do right now. I'm set for life. I have three homes. All my kids are through college. One of them's a lawyer and I'll make sure he helps you if you ever need an attorney. But getting back to the house . . . just sit down here."

I sat down and he said, "I'm going to write you a check for seven hundred dollars." It was a good thing I *was* sitting down. I said, "I got no way of paying you back. Maybe you could take twenty dollars out of my salary every week." He said, "Now wait a minute. I don't want you to consider that you're borrowing this money. This is what you call for services rendered. Maybe I even should have done this a couple of years ago. It's because you've been very good to this department. You did things in this department with people and to people that nobody else could accomplish."

I sat right there and I cried. I said to myself, "Gee whiz, this man really cares about me and about my wife and my son, and about whether we get this house or not. Here's someone who really went out of his way to help us."

So I went home. And Sue and I both sat on the side of the bed and cried.

And that's how the Colemans acquired the very first home they ever had and became the first black family in a previously all-white neighborhood.

The Millers came to visit and to play with Gary every time they returned to Zion.

Willie tried three times, over the years, to repay the seven hundred dollars to Dr. Close, but he would never accept the money.

9

The Colemans settled into their new house and it was a happy time for a while. Gary flourished in the new environment. The Colemans bought Gary a German shepherd puppy, Champion, who became his constant companion as they grew up together. The white children in the neighborhood took to Gary immediately because of his irresistible gregariousness, so there were plenty of playmates. Three special friends were the children of Judy Fritz, Dr. Woroch's secretary, who often asked Willie to bring Gary over to play.

The new house had a spacious basement room, in which Gary began to accumulate small electric models of the trains that had first begun to fascinate him when he was an infant in Willie's parents' home in Lima. The space age was long since under way, and while Gary watched and read everything he could about the astronauts (he was reading quite proficiently at the age of four, before he started school), trains remained his consuming interest. Willie used to take him to watch the big diesels roll by on their way to and from Chicago.

With Sue's parents happily retired in a lovely house back in Lima, Willie and Sue, when their vacation times coincided, could now drive the child to visit all his grandparents in the same Ohio city. Grandpa Lovelace knew all the fishing lakes, and great story teller that he is, beguiled the little boy with tales of his fox-hunting days in Alabama. Grandma Coleman still lived by the railroad tracks. Gary spent hours in her house watching the mile-long freight trains rumble past. Willie took him to the vast Lima switching yards, and soon the four-year-old was startling adults by rattling off the names of the different types of diesel engines—"the SD-40s, SD-45s, GP-9s, RS-11s and GP-38s."

Much later, one of the most startled adults ever confronted by Gary was Dinah Shore, on whose TV talk show he was a guest. Not only did Gary accurately name the SD-40s, and so on, but he informed her and her audience about all the railroad lines that ran through Lima—the Pennsylvania, The Nickel Plate, the Chesapeake and Ohio, the Baltimore and Ohio, the Norfolk and Western. He even remembered the little D.T. and I., the Detroit, Toledo and Ironton. Since some of these lines are not even in existence now, the memory has to come from those early days of his childhood.

When Gary was five, he began kindergarten at the Shiloh Park School near their new house in Zion. The first day of school was an even more anxious one

A GIFT OF LIFE

for Sue than it ordinarily is for most parents. She had to go to see the principal, an understanding and compassionate young man named Robert Fink, to explain to him about Gary's pouch. Mr. Fink told her that all Gary had to do was raise his hand whenever he wanted to empty the pouch, and all teachers would be instructed to allow him to go to the bathroom immediately.

The amazing thing is that none of the other children even suspected that Gary had any kind of disability. He always managed to accomplish his pouch-emptying without anyone else noticing. The only potential problem arose after the first few days when Mr. Fink called Sue at work to report that her son was so bright and personable that the other children took to him immediately, but that the kids were rough-housing it up pretty good in the playground. Sue urged caution, but told Fink not to worry. She had gone through the same anxieties watching Gary at play with other children in her own backyard.

Fink says, "I never worried about Gary's medical problems after that. He was tough, resourceful and a survivor. Knowing his parents, I guess that he inherited those qualities from them. And I was amazed at his natural intelligence. He could read and write, actually print, at third-grade level. He was ahead of most of the other kindergarteners—black *and* white—and was a natural leader from the very beginning. Even when he had to take a day or two off to go for his checkups at the hospital, he never had any trouble keeping abreast of the rest of the class."

But Gary's medical problems were building up, and Sue and Willie were painfully aware of them.

It began with calcium "clubbing," knobs that sprouted on Gary's wrists and ankles, causing discomfort and sometimes inhibiting easy movement of his hands and feet. With a slowly failing kidney, such as Gary's remaining damaged one, there is a leakage of calcium and phosphates. Since calcium, in particular, is necessary for building bone in a still-growing child, Sue had been charged with administering calcium tablets to Gary every day. The idea is to replace the calcium that is just spilling out of the kidney and not being utilized in bone growth by the body.

Unfortunately, much of the calcium given to Gary by Sue was not making its way into the bone. Instead, it was building up into those knobs. The doctors at Children's Memorial instructed Sue to give Gary daily dosages of vitamin D. The knobs disappeared, but the episode left Sue disturbed about what was going on inside Gary's little body.

The doctors were anxious, too. By now, the nephrology team had been joined by the skilled young kidney transplant surgeon, Dr. Casimir Firlit, who had been a Navy doctor in the Vietnam war and then accumulated experience in transplantation as a urology resident at the Veterans Administration and Loyola University hospitals. Dr. Firlit concurred with the others that Gary's kidney now was failing at a much more rapid rate. It had dropped from forty percent function to less than twenty percent. When the kidney was only five percent operative, it would have to be removed or the child would die. Gary had to be prepared now, either for dialysis or, if he were fortunate enough to have a donor kidney available, for a transplant.

A GIFT OF LIFE

Gary's monthly trips to the hospital became more lengthy and traumatic. Entering through the penis with their instruments, the doctors cut away the congenital flaps in the urethra (actually undeveloped valves) which had caused the obstruction. Then, because the bladder had been disconnected and not used by Gary for more than three years, they periodically pumped antibiotic fluids into it, also through the penis, to prevent infection and to condition the bladder to expand to its normal size. All this was painful, and though he never cried, the hospital visits were no longer fun for Gary.

In the meantime, Dr. Firlit and Dr. Lewy carefully scanned the creatinine levels in Gary's blood samples. Creatinine is a crucial waste product in the blood which is normally removed by the glomerulus and the tubule in each of the million nephrons in the kidney. If the creatinine slips past the nephrons and returns to the bloodstream instead of being excreted in the urine, it provides a reliable measure of the percentage of nonfunction of the kidney tissue.

By November 1973, Gary's creatinine level had nearly reached that lethal point where only five percent of the kidney was working.

Gary, Willie and Sue were called in to see the doctors during the Thanksgiving weekend. The entire scenario was laid out for them. Within two months at the most, Gary probably would have to go on a dialysis machine. That meant two or three days a week in the hospital. It meant immobility and little chance to continue normally at school. It meant that Willie's career, and also Sue's, would be seriously threatened by the many, many trips to the hospital. Also, because the science of dialysis had not reached the effectiveness it now has, Gary would be chronically and seriously debilitated.

Transplantation seemed out of the question. There were few donors in those days, before the public awareness later stimulated by the National Kidney Foundation. Dr. Firlit briefly considered the idea of Sue donating one of her kidneys, but quickly discarded the notion. The blood and tissue match was excellent, but there had been little experience, until then, in transplanting an adult kidney into a small child and it was considered dangerous to try. Today, it is known that a large man's kidney can be transplanted even into a newborn infant. But in 1973, the state of the art had not advanced that far.

So the Colemans went home—to worry, and to wait, and to pray.

10

On December 7, 1973, a six-year-old boy we'll call Adam was playing in the front yard of his suburban northern Indiana home. He was a white child, with the handsome Slavic features and blond hair of his eastern European ancestry.

As he worked on building a snowman, Adam suddenly saw his grandfather across the street, laden with bags of groceries from the market. Adam started across the street to help his grandfather with the groceries. There was a screech of brakes, and Adam was hit head-on by a car, which halted momentarily but then sped on, a clear case of hit-and-run.

Adam was rushed to the local hospital. He had several broken bones, but the main problem was severe head injuries. He never regained consciousness. An angiogram determined that, at the very least, he was suffering a subdural hematoma, a massive blood clot between two of the tissues that enclose the brain. He needed immediate neurosurgery, and the best pediatric neurosurgeons were at Children's Memorial Hospital, about 70 miles away in Chicago. A paramedic helicopter was called and the boy was flown to Meigs Field, where an ambulance was waiting to speed him to Children's Memorial.

At the hospital, one brain surgery was performed, then another. And another. Adam remained in a coma for eight days, kept alive only by artificial life support systems. On December 15, Adam's distraught father knew his son was going to die. He asked to see someone in the hospital's nephrology team. He was escorted to Dr. Firlit's office.

Dr. Firlit says today, "It was one of the most incredible experiences of my life, then or since. The man said, 'I know my son isn't going to make it. I also know you're doing valuable work here in kidney transplants. I want to donate both of my son's kidneys to give life to two other children.' I was astounded. Usually, in those days, we had the painful job of approaching the parents of dying children and appealing to them to donate organs. Today with the public better educated it's easier, but then, more often than not, we were turned down.

"I thanked the man passionately and I told him that both the law and medical ethics require that there be total anonymity about Adam's kidneys and who would receive them," Dr. Firlit continued. "I explained that the information about the kidneys would be fed into a central computer at the university of Illinois. The computer would then match the tissue and blood types with all children in the Midwest awaiting a transplant. I told him that Adam's kidneys might even end up in children as far away as Montreal or New Orleans. The man said he understood and shook hands and left. My heart went out to him but there was nothing more I could say but thanks. What I pointedly did *not* explain to him in his anguish was that the reason for anonymity was to prevent the selling of kidneys and profiting on sorrow."

Adam died that night. Almost immediately his kidneys were surgically removed. The kidneys would die within fifteen minutes if they were to remain at body temperature, so they were washed in a cool isotonic salt solution and then placed in a portable eighty-pound preservation device called a Belzer Machine. In essence, the device is a pump that delivers food, oxygen, and an acid-base balance to the kidney. By lowering the temperature to about 40 degrees Fahrenheit, the machine keeps the kidney in a state of hypothermic (low temperature) hibernation for up to 96 hours. This is usually enough time for the centralized computer to find a suitable recipient. Also, the machine is portable and battery-operated, so it can be flown to a distant city, if necessary, within the 96 hours.

Dr. Firlit says, "The lymph nodes from the donor kidney are removed for tissue-typing at the University of Illinois labs and when I sent them off in this case, I had no idea that I would get both kidneys back. At the lab, they already have all information about potential recipients in their computer. They check for the best possible match with the donated kidneys—blood type, how many antigens they share, what we call a 'lymphocytotic crossmatch,' which tells us whether or not the recipient has certain antibodies in his system which will immediately reject the transplant. There are so many combinations and possibilities of mismatches, that I was absolutely amazed when the University of Illinois people called me and said, 'OK, keep them. You've got the two most promising recipients right there.' They were Gary and the little three-year-old boy from Tennessee, Chandel."

That's how Sue Coleman came to receive the unexpected phone call from Dr. Firlit on the morning of December 18, 1973, leading to the family's mad dash to Children's Memorial, and Sue's long nighttime reverie in the parents' waiting room as the transplant operation on Gary proceeded.

11

Sue's waiting-room recollections ended abruptly at about 11:30 P.M. when a young intern came through the waiting room and told her that Gary was doing OK and everything was going as expected.

Gary now was in the fifth hour of the operation.

Sue looked around the waiting room and noted that everyone else was asleep. She looked at her watch. It would be another half hour before two of the parents would be awakened to see their children in the intensive care unit. They were allowed a ten minute visit every two hours. For those, like herself, who had children still in surgery, there would be no break in the waiting.

Sue

Wide awake now, my eye fell on Willie. He was stretched out on a cot, fast asleep. I marveled at how different we were. Willie loved Gary just as much as I did, but he could sleep in his exhaustion and I couldn't. Maybe Willie had more faith than I did. The last thing Gary told us before being wheeled away was, "Now, I'm going to come through this fine, so I don't want either one of you to do any weepin' and wailin' and worryin' while you're out there in the waiting room." Willie took this almost as an order. Earlier, he got into an argument with the Oriental couple who *were* weepin' and wailin'. They asked how he could be so calm at a time like this. Willie said, "Because my son told me to, that's why."

Then, as now, I realized we had a good marriage, Willie and I. As with all good marriages, we have our conflicts. For one thing, I guess I nagged him pretty good about going back to school for his diploma. In the end, he did it, but it was his own decision. As I said, he's a proud and independent man.

He makes me mad sometimes; he's overpowering sometimes; he's domineering sometimes. He's the kind of person you can't tell anything to—you say it's green, he says no, it's blue. But he's the one you go to when you really need someone to talk to, because he really understands the practicality of any given situation.

And he's decisive. I always can come home and talk to him and he understands why it's important to me.

On the other hand, he gets mad at me sometimes because he may be carrying on about something and I will not talk. He'll say, "You've been sitting there all day and you haven't said a word." In fact, I may be brooding. Or I may be procrastinating. I don't enjoy making decisions, which drives him crazy. We had lots of arguments on one of his job situations. He ended by throwing up his hands and yelling, "I ask you, and I ask you, and I ask you—and you don't give me any answers." I said to him, "You decide things by instinct. You just know and feel that something is right. It takes me a little longer; I have to try to see it from both sides, weigh the advantages and disadvantages. But we always eventually end up on the same wave length, don't we?" He agreed, and the fight was over.

On that note, I dozed for a while, until the same young intern came in and told me again that Gary was doing OK and everything was going as expected.

Inside the operating room, the complicated surgery was proceeding as smoothly as possible under the circumstances—the circumstances being that a nephrectomy, the surgical removal of a kidney, rarely takes place at the same time as transplantation of a new donor kidney. Usually, the old kidney has long since been removed and the patient has been on dialysis while awaiting the availability of a donor kidney.

Dr. Firlit did the surgery. He was assisted by Dr.

Belman, by a young resident, and by two operating-room nurses. As Dr. Firlit describes the operation, the long incision was made and the body cavity exposed. "There was his kidney," says Dr. Firlit, "and it was very small. We clamped off the two main blood vessels, the renal artery and the renal vein, and then we simply lifted out the kidney and its conduit, the ureter. It came out very easily, so we did the whole thing in one fell swoop."

In the meantime, the new kidney was in its preservation machine, off to one side, just inside the operating room door. The kidney had been removed from its donor with the artery, vein and ureter still attached. It was a right kidney, which according to practice would be implanted in Gary's left side. The trickiest part of the operation is preparing the site for the new kidney. It does not go back into the old site, behind the lower ribs, but down in front in the lower part of the abdomen. "The reason for this," say Dr. Firlit, "is twofold. First, it lies just beneath the skin and outside the peritoneum—the membrane which encloses the intestines and other abdominal organs—which makes it much easier for the doctor to examine the kidney later on. You can feel the organ through the skin, test it for size, consistency, and tenderness of the surrounding tissue, and your fingers alone give you a pretty good idea of what is going on. The second reason for putting it down there in the lower abdomen is to shorten the distance the urine has to travel down the ureter from the kidney to the bladder. The ureter has a very poor blood supply, so the shorter the distance the better. We've learned that without blood, as much as half the original length of the ureter can die."

A GIFT OF LIFE

So a pocket was constructed surgically in Gary's lower left side. Then the preservation machine was wheeled over. The new kidney was taken out of the machine and carefully placed in the pocket. It settled perfectly into the cavity. Then came the tedious task of attaching and sewing up the renal artery and the renal vein.

The final test was when the clamps were released and the blood flow resumed to the new kidney. "It's miraculous what you then see with a very good kidney," Dr. Firlit says. The kidney, which is pale and soft, suddenly becomes pink and firm. In a matter of minutes you can actually watch it manufacturing urine. You can see the ureter tensing itself up and relaxing—what we call peristaltic action—and then urine drips out of the end of the ureter before you connect it to the bladder. Sometimes the urine shoots out like a jet. It wasn't that spectacular in Gary's case—just a nice steady flow—but it was good enough to make us want to cheer."

Sue

It was just about 1:30 in the morning when Dr. Firlit came into the waiting room. He leaned against the door and beckoned us over. His eyes were glowing and I've never seen someone on such a natural high.

"Gary's fantastic," he said, and he told us

all about how the new kidney turned pink and started to manufacture urine right away. He must have carried that excitement-high with him directly from the operating room. Though we didn't know exactly what he was talking about at the time, we knew it was good news. A buzz of excitement went around the room, as if the other parents were hearing about their own kids. The doctor told us, "Gary's in the recovery room now. I stayed with him until he woke up from the anesthesia. Do you know the first thing he said when he was awake?" We said "What?" He said, " '*Now* can I have a drink of water?' "

This may have been the first laugh Gary ever got from an audience, because we had told the parents in the waiting room about how Gary had kept trying to get a drink of water before the operation. The others not only laughed but crowded around us to shake our hands and Dr. Firlit's. Dr. Firlit said, "Excuse me, but I still have to transplant the second kidney into the other child." And he was gone.

I was so giddy by now that I don't exactly remember how long it was before they let us go in to see Gary in Intensive Care. He was lying in his bed with one of those plastic globes over his head—what they call the "oxygen bubble." He was still drifting in and out of sleep, but he recognized us right away and he said, "Am I in outer space, Mommy?"

That got a pretty good laugh, too, from Toni Greenslade and the other nurses on the floor.

But the biggest laugh of all came the next day—or was it the same day?—when I called my parents in Lima to tell them the operation had taken place and everything seemed to be OK. Gary insisted on getting on the phone "to talk to Grandpa." We gave him the phone and he bellowed, loud enough for everyone on the floor to hear, "Grandpa, I can pee through my peepee!"

Much later, Toni Greenslade said, "We all laughed, but then when we thought about the meaning of what the child had said, the abnormal life he had led for four years, some of us didn't feel like laughing anymore."

12

There wasn't much laughter at all over the next three days in the hospital. That's the period when the greatest number of rejections occur. Simply put, rejection of a transplanted kidney occurs when the body's natural defense systems—lymphocytes, white blood cells, antibodies—perceive the new kidney as a foreign invader. They attack it and try to destroy it, just as they would a disease organism that has invaded the body.

Science has learned how to inhibit these natural body defenses by giving the patient large doses of steroids and other so-called immunosuppressive drugs. The drugs, in effect, hold back the defense forces until the new organ establishes itself and the dosages can be reduced to the point where the defenders no longer attack the kidney but do resume their normal function of fighting off diseases.

A GIFT OF LIFE

In those first three days, Gary was monitored almost constantly by the doctors and nurses in the hospital. It was the same with Chandel, the young child who received what is called "the mate" to Gary's new kidney. Gary thrived; Chandel did not.

Dr. Firlit shakes his head sadly when he recalls the two cases. "We reach a certain amount of sophistication in our surgery and our postoperative techniques," he says, "and we think we've done everything perfectly. Yet I always say it's the Great Big Transplanter in the Sky who makes it work. With Gary and Chandel, for instance, both patients were handled the same way, they both had the same probability of success. But Gary was fine; and the other child suffered early rejection, complications from that point on, and eventual death. I had another situation just like that, a boy and a girl who shared the same donor. The girl came through marvelously, the boy didn't. So who's to know? With some remarkable new advances being made, we may look back on kidney transplantation ten years from now and consider *this* period to be the Dark Ages."

The critical three days came and went, and Gary continued to do well. He was hungry and talkative, and he showed absolutely no symptoms of rejection. The next critical point would be in three weeks.

Willie went home to Zion, but returned several nights to spell Sue at Gary's bedside. At Abbott, he learned of some heartwarming developments. There had been prayer meetings for Gary in all of the local churches attended by Abbott employees. Also, there was an enormous collection of toys for Willie to haul down to Gary in the hospital. The hauling was the most difficult part. Each trip to Chicago was costing him four dollars in gasoline (a pittance compared with today), and Willie was hard-pressed to afford it. Being a proud man, he told nobody, but worked a few hours overtime and on Saturdays to earn the extra money.

Gary

I remember Dad coming in every other day with so many toys that they overflowed the bed and nearly buried me, but I can only remember parts and pieces of everything that happened since the day I came to the hospital for the transplant and they gave me that dumb red balloon that I blowed up and it made me pass out. I guess I don't recall coming out of the operation because they gave me a lot of stuff to take because of the pain.

I also don't remember much at all about the first three days, except for the pain and that I was very hungry but an old bow-legged nurse with yellow hair wouldn't give me anything to eat but mush. I had a bubble plastic over my head at first, and I remember seeing Mom and Dad through it. But then they had a whole plastic tent over my bed. That dumb old nurse told me that was because I was very susceptible to germs then and no one could come near me so I wouldn't get infected. When she came with my food, she pushed it through a little flap in the plastic, and when Mom and Dad came to see me, they could only reach in and touch me through that same flap.

Then things got to get better. The pain began to go away and they took the tent off my bed. That dumb old nurse with the yellow hair gave me all the food I wanted, even steaks, and I was allowed to get up and share that big crazy pile of toys with the other kids. I played checkers with them. Then Toni Greenslade came in and said I could go to the playroom, where there was a lot of neat electronic games. I had a lot of fun there, when they weren't hauling me hither and yon for all kinds of blood tests and scans and like that.

I like Toni Greenslade best of all the people in the hospital. She was just a floor nurse then, but now she's almost a doctor. I remember that she came in one day after the operation with some crayons and drawing paper. She told me to make pictures that she could hang up on her wall. I had a lot of fun drawing my favorite trains and cars.

One night a police siren woke me up, so the next morning I decided to draw a police car. Toni came in and she said, "Why is that police car brown, instead of black-and-white or blue-and-white or green-and-white?" I said, "This police car is brown because it's under cover." Toni laughed and hugged me, and my under-cover police car is still hanging up on the wall of her office.

In the hospital, as Gary got through those first critical three weeks seemingly without incident, Sue received endless briefings on the additional home nursing duties she would have to assume when he was released.

Sue

The first thing they impressed on me was the importance of Gary getting his immunosuppressive drugs every day, without fail. After a while, the new kidney might be recognized by the defense cells in his body as *not* an enemy. But the only sure way to prevent rejection is for the patient to take the steroids and the other medications daily—for life. They explained that it was just like a diabetic needing daily insulin all his life, in order to survive.

They told me the principal drugs I would be giving Gary were Prednisone and Imuran. They said science did not really know how and why they worked, but that they had been very successful in preventing kidney-transplant rejection since about 1963. They warned me that they'd be constantly varying the dosage of the drugs, and that I'd have to keep accurate charts of every ounce of fluid Gary drank, compared with every ounce of fluid he urinated. The idea of varying the doses was to counter anything abnormal that might be going on in the kidney. But even more important, they wanted to get the dosage down to the delicate balance where it was just enough to prevent rejection of the kidney while still being enough to fight off disease.

They told me I had to keep Gary's diet almost salt-free. No more of the potato chips and corn chips he loved. They also shook me up by saying

I'd have to go through potty-training all over again with Gary. "Don't forget," they said, "that he hasn't used his bladder for four years now. He's going to have to learn how to hold his urine in, until he can get to a toilet, just like he was taught to do as a baby. Also, the bladder is going to hurt him for a while as it fills up. After all, it's elastic tissue and it's been a long time since it's been stretched."

The doctors then gave me their most difficult news which I already knew, in a way. They said that Gary would always be small. They said that this happens with nearly all children, almost without exception, who receive transplants before they finish growing. That's why it's better to wait, if possible, until the teenage years.

The doctors explained that when the calcium and phosphorus leakage occurs with the original kidney disease, the growth process slows down or stops. I knew that because of the calcium supplements I'd been giving Gary since the second operation. But, the doctors added, the steroids Gary now had to take every day also interfere with growth. Again, it was one of those phenomena which is not understood. We don't know why the steroids inhibit growth. But as Dr. Firlit said, "It's better to be short and have a kidney than to be tall and *not* have a kidney."

I asked, "How short?" They didn't know. I'd have to give Gary calcium and phosphorus with his daily medication, and they'd be able to tell better later on. They said some children with transplants do have growth spurts, including a dramatic one sometimes at puberty, which is usually delayed in these kids.

I sensed that the doctors didn't really want to talk beyond the first six months after the operation, which is the next big plateau in the fight against rejection.

So we discussed such immediate problems as sutures that might pop out of Gary's incision after he came home, and did I know how to take care of them to prevent infection, and so on, without having to rush him to the hospital every time?

I said I did. Then I asked them, "Is there a time, like in cancer, where after five years you're considered to have licked it? Is there a time when you figure a transplanted kidney has pretty much made it?"

"Yes," they said. "Two years."

Dr. Lewy qualifies this statement. "The rule of thumb is that after two years we don't usually have to worry about acute rejection any more. Slow, chronic rejection can still occur, but that we can manage."

In the meantime, though, it was still one day at a time for Gary in that first three-week period in the hospital. His incisions healed nicely and the kidney kept functioning as if he had had it in his body all his life. There was no leakage, no tenderness, no unduly high levels of creatinine or any other waste product in the blood. He spent his days playing happily with his new bonanza of toys and sharing them with the other children. He wrote poems and drew pictures for Toni Greenslade's bulletin board.

Sue was exhausted but delighted at Gary's daily physical progress. She was not aware of some of the occasional mystical side effects that accompany kidney transplantation—both for the children and their parents.

Dr. Ira Greifer of the Kidney Foundation explains, "There's something about the kidney transplant, a feeling of acquiring temporary immortality perhaps, that causes people to do and think strange things. It doesn't happen with corneal transplants; on the other hand, it probably will happen when heart transplants become feasible and common. It has to do with getting a gift of life, which is the slogan of our organization.

"So we have children waking up with nightmares, wondering who they are. We have children dreaming in terror about the donor child returning to take the kidney back. We have parents who are driven to breach our secrecy regulations and try desperately to find out who the donor was, much like an adopted child searching for its natural parents. We had one tragic case, where a boy inadvertently learned that his kidney came from the father he hated, and the child jumped out the hospital window and committed suicide. There's a psychologist in Minneapolis, Roberta Simmons, who has devoted herself to these phenomena and the psychological adjustments that must be made in some transplantation cases."

Gary, happily, has remained immune to any of these aberrations, but strangely, it was strong, quiet, unflappable Sue who became a victim.

It came about in a strange way. "It's possible she heard gossip in the hospital cafeteria—try as we might we can't stop that—" Dr. Firlit says, "but she came away with the impression that the donor child in Gary's case was of Greek descent."

Then, on Christmas Eve, Sue was approached in the hospital waiting room by a distraught young woman dressed in black.

Sue

This woman was Mediterranean-looking with dark hair and pale skin. She had obviously been crying. Timidly she asked me if she could go in to see Gary for a few minutes. She said she wanted to give him a little present. I said sure, and she went into the ward for a while and then left. Gary had so many toys by that time that I was never sure which one she had given him.

What I *was* sure of was that this lady was the Greek-American mother of the little boy who was killed and gave Gary the "gift of life." For seven years I kept thinking about her. I wondered how to get in touch with her. I wanted to thank her, to mourn with her, to try to help alleviate *her* pain. Then I'd think to myself, "No, I can't invade her privacy. I'll have to wait until she approaches me again." It was a ghost I lived with for a long, long time.

The ghost was not laid to rest until Dr. Firlit first became aware of the problem during the research for this book.

Dr. Firlit told Sue, "It was absolutely impossible

A GIFT OF LIFE

for that woman to have been the mother of the boy who was the kidney donor in Gary's case. It had to have been some other bereaved parent who had simply seen Gary in the ward and fallen in love with him, as nearly everyone else did."

Asked how he could be so sure, Dr. Firlit said, "Because the little boy who was the donor was not Greek or Mediterranean, and because the very real fact is that he *had* no mother. She was long since dead."

13

For Gary, there was still one more medical crisis to come.

Over the next few months, however, the Colemans enjoyed more normal, routine living than they had known since the first day of his illness. They had a completely whole child again.

Gary came home from the hospital early in January 1974. Except for his weekly checkups at Children's Memorial, which could be done on Saturdays, there was no longer any external evidence that anything had been wrong.

The only dislocations fell on Sue, and she bore her new burdens with her usual stoicism. It was her responsibility now to make sure that Gary took as many as eight different medications a day: the immunosuppressives and the dietary supplements. The dosages had to be administered to the exact number of milligrams prescribed by the doctors. If she

A GIFT OF LIFE

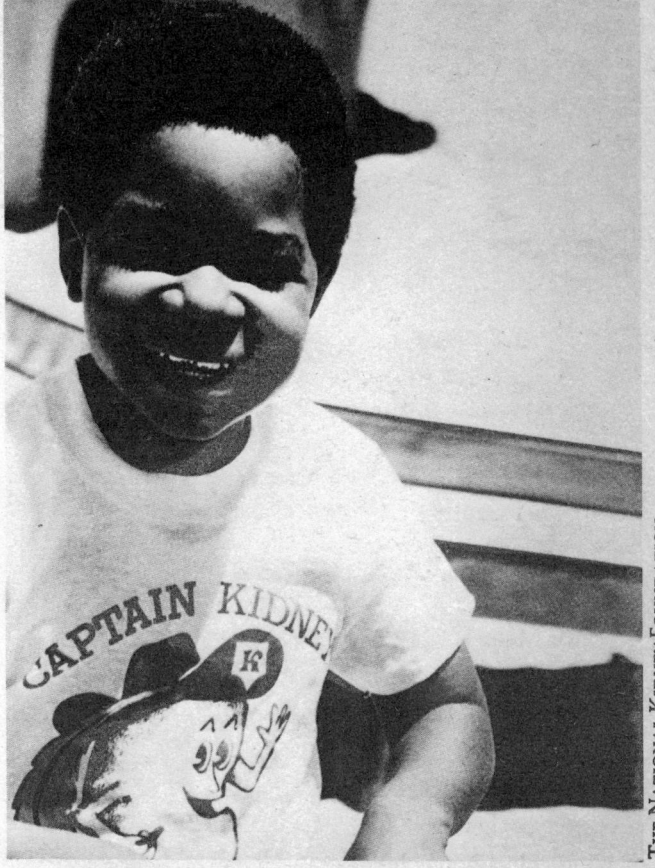

THE NATIONAL KIDNEY FOUNDATION

Gary preparing to do a TV commercial for the National Kidney Foundation. "We wanted to let other people see Gary as an example of how a kidney transplant can work. We wanted to encourage other parents who get so frightened," Sue says.

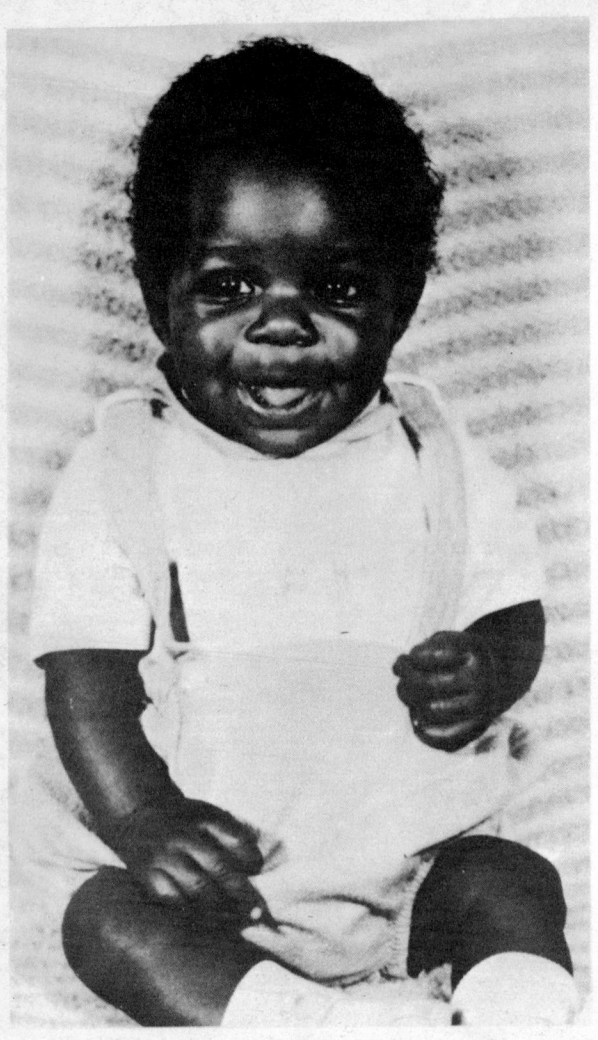

Willie and Sue found that they had an energetic and extremely bright son.

Sue at twenty-two.

Willie at twenty-nine.

Gary celebrates his transplanted kidney's seventh birthday at a party at Children's Hospital in Los Angeles. Sue and Willie said, "Do you realize what a lucky kid you are? Most other kids get presents once at this time of year. You're going to get them twice—on the kidney's birthday and on Christmas Day."

On the set of **Scout's Honor**. *Top:* Gary and actor Pat O'Brien share their interest in trains. *Bottom:* Sue, Gary and Willie during filming.

"If you ask me if I'd rather be short and smart or tall and dumb, I'd have to say, 'I'll take tall and smart.' But now I realize that I don't have any control over that so I'll take it like it is."

Right: "With all his vitality," Sue says, "it's easy to forget that Gary is a chronically ill child. Any child with a kidney transplant is chronically ill, even though it never shows on the surface."

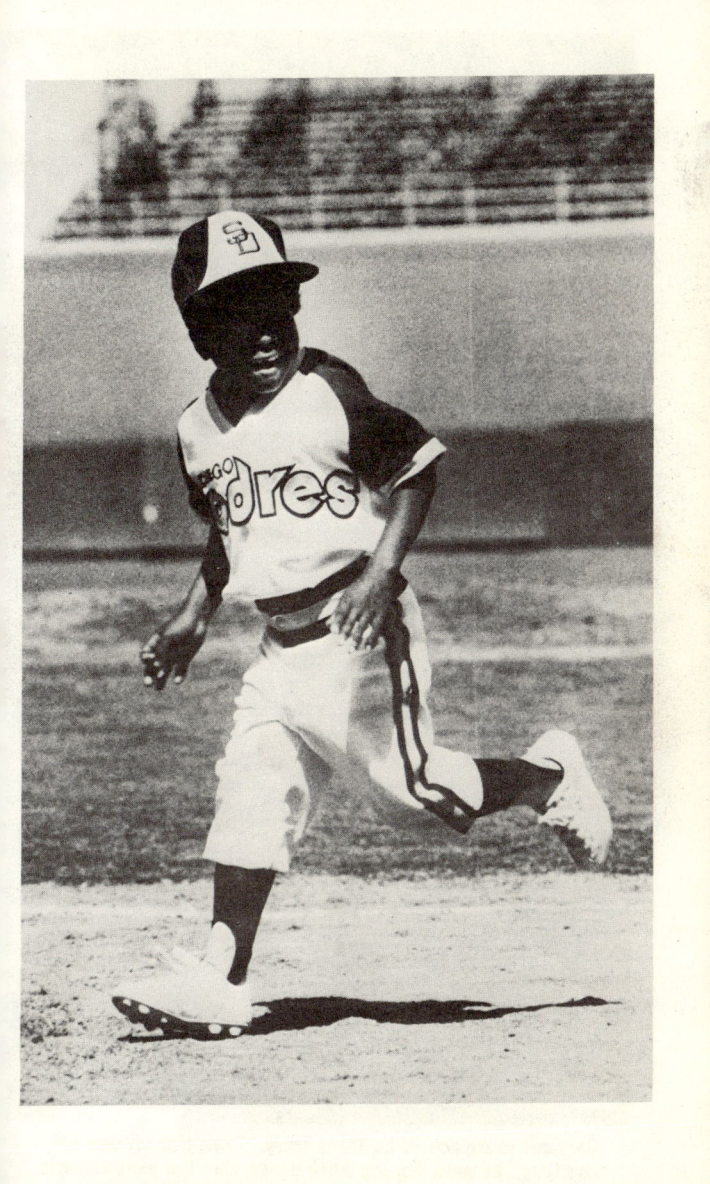

Gary and his pet chihuahua, Venus, romp with an unknown friend.

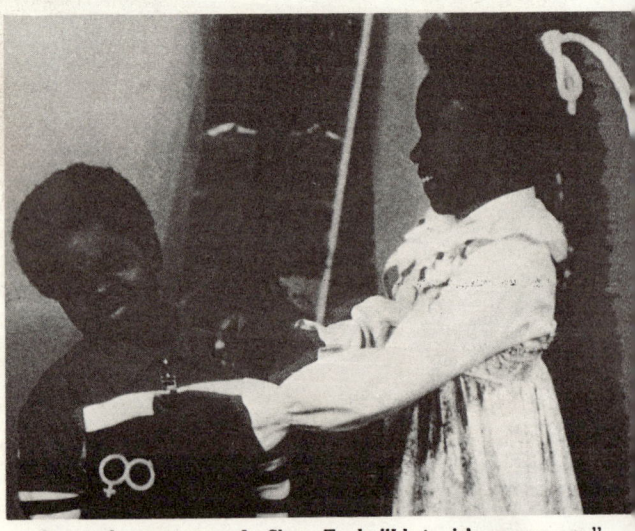

Gary and young actress La Shana Tendy. "I hate girls my own age," says Gary, "because they say dumb things, like, 'I'm going to marry you for your money.'"

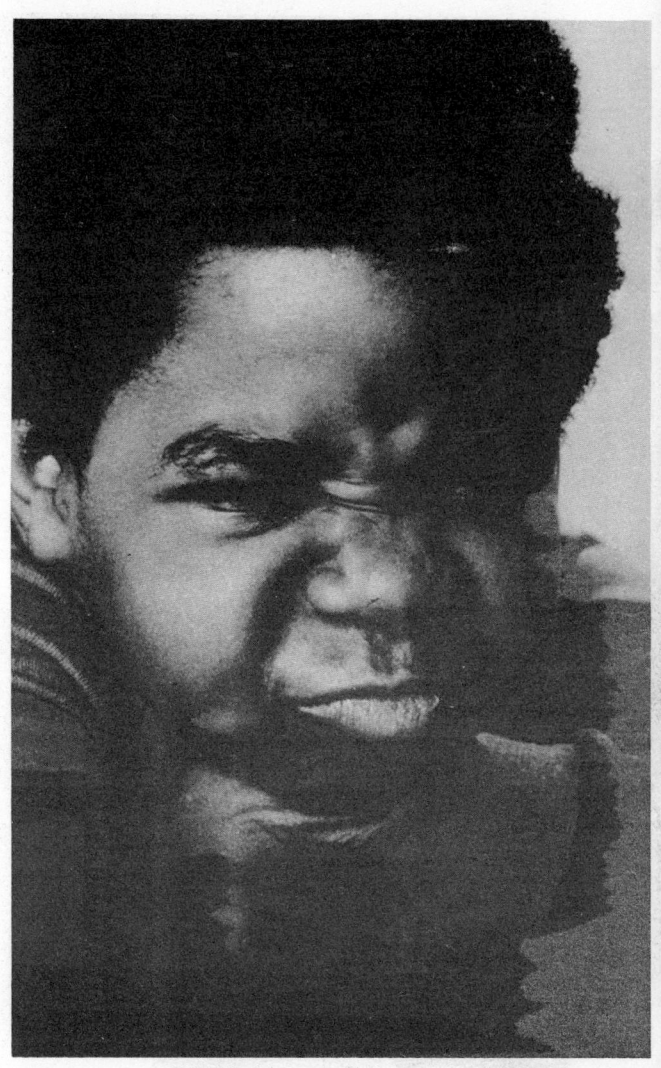

"I like to make people laugh."

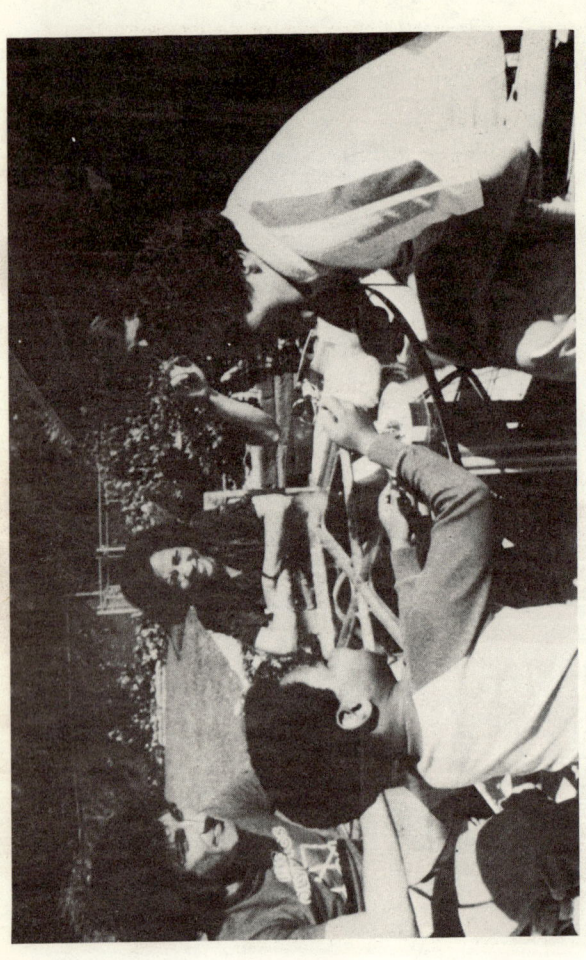

Gary with the strategists of his own production company, Zephyr Productions. *Left to right:* Lawyer Harry Sloan, Sue, lawyer Lawrence Kuppin and agent Vic Perillo.

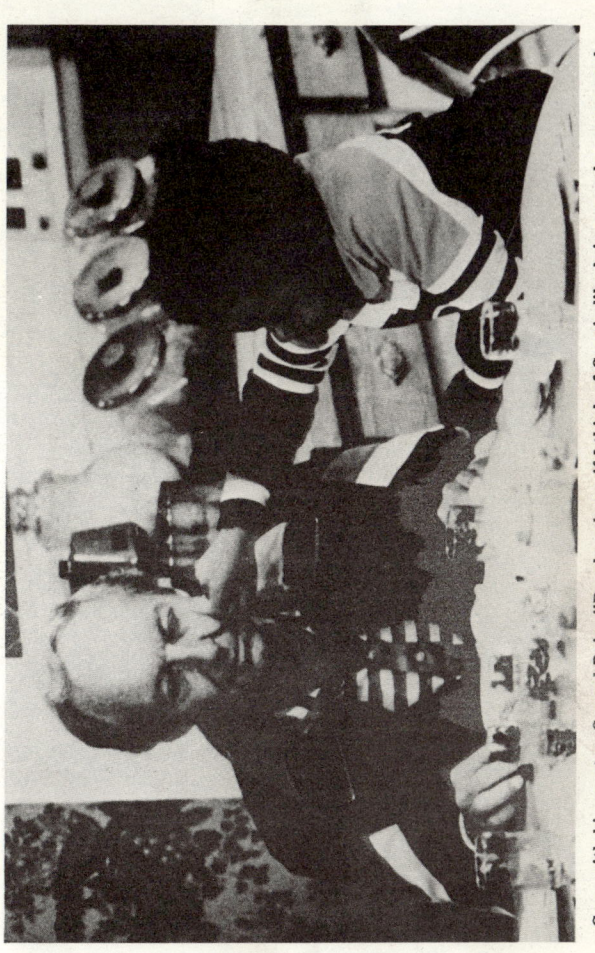

Gary with his co-star, Conrad Bain. "People ask me if I think of Connie like he's a grandpa or an uncle, but none of those things are right. He's more a best friend, like your cat or your dog. Only he can talk."

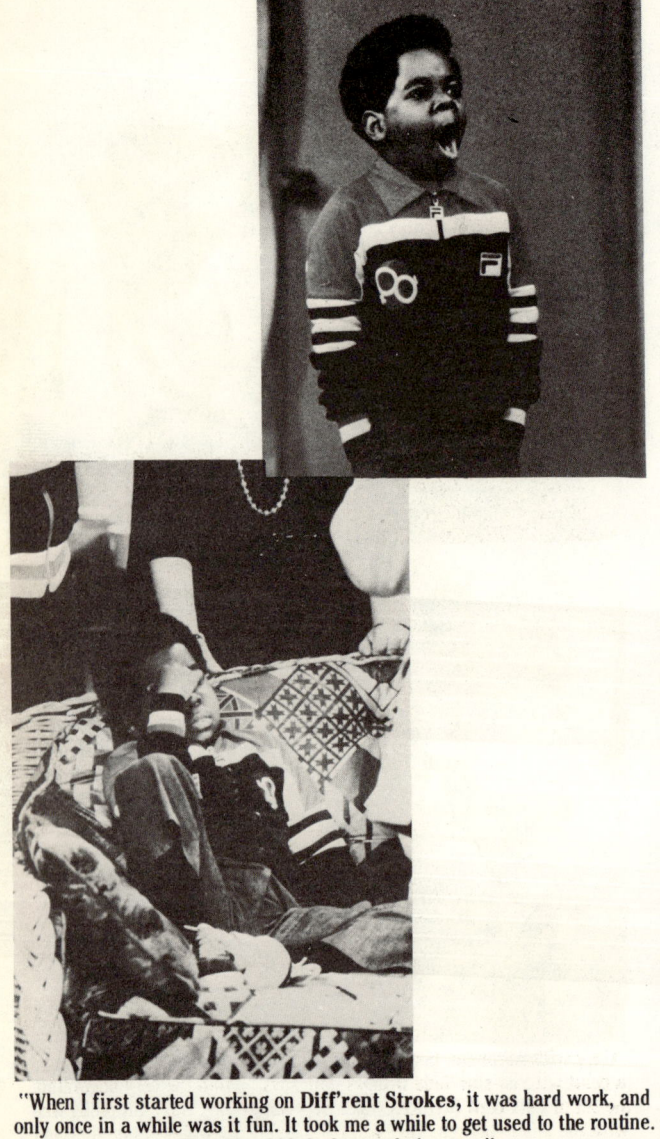

"When I first started working on **Diff'rent Strokes**, it was hard work, and only once in a while was it fun. It took me a while to get used to the routine. The other kids had a tough time too."

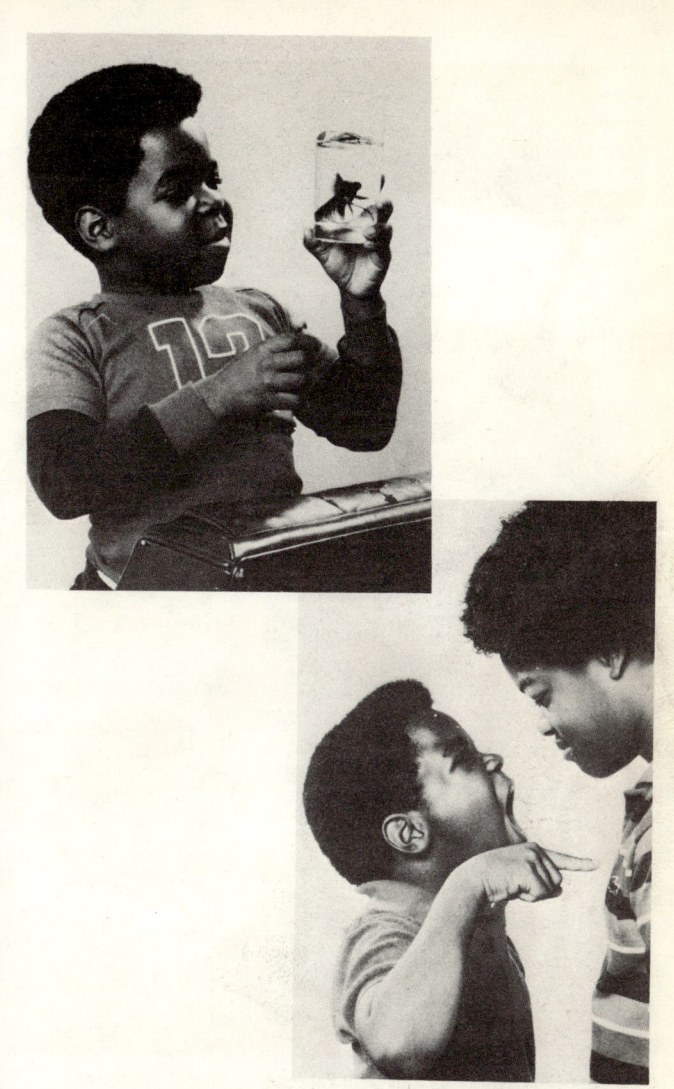

Gary with Abraham, his pet fish on **Diff'rent Strokes**; and arguing a point with co-star Todd Bridges. Sue says, "From the very beginning, the set of **Diff'rent Strokes** was a very happy one. Gary got along well with the other children. They worked together, they played together and they went to school together."

Top: Gary shares his train with Pat Paulsen, whom he succeeded as spokesman for the National Kidney Foundation. *Bottom:* A break in filming his first big screen movie, **On the Right Track**, with co-star Lisa Eilbacher.

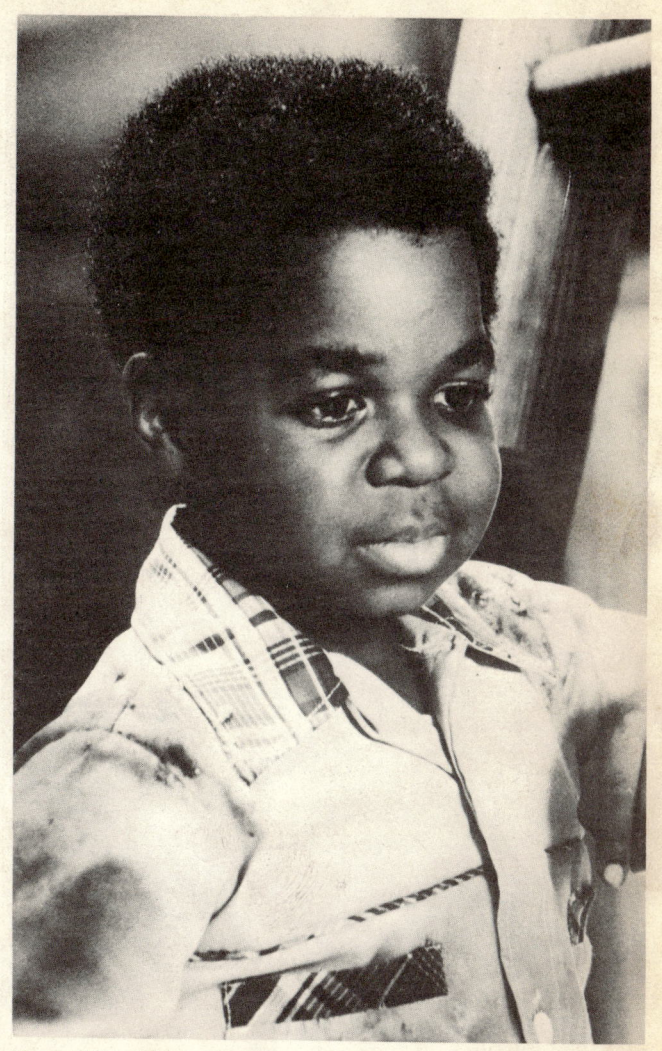

The word 'genius' keeps popping up in Gary's many guest appearances with such talk-show hosts as Johnny Carson and Merv Griffin.

Gary's former principal, Robert Fink, says, "He was tough, resourceful and a survivor. Knowing his parents, I guess he inherited those qualities from them."

detected anything in the least abnormal in Gary, such as a headache, which might be attributed to an elevation in blood pressure as the new kidney adjusted, she'd immediately call Dr. Lewy or Dr. Firlit and they'd make temporary dosage changes over the telephone until the next weekly checkup. Between checkups, too, Sue had to measure the intake and outflow of fluids and to keep tabs on the incisions so that when a suture worked its way to the surface, she could clean the area with antiseptics. The sutures kept "popping" for months. Even with her resumption of night nursing duty at her own hospital, Sue considered all this nothing compared with what she had been through before.

Only one thing troubled her during this period, Sue recalls, and that was a mother's reaction, not a nurse's. She would hear Gary cry out in his sleep as his bladder filled, causing pain in the tissue which still had not attained its normal elasticity. Since Gary rarely cried, she'd run to the child's room to awaken him to go to the bathroom. She did that only a few times. Then Gary, not wanting to disturb and upset his parents, conditioned himself to wake up at the first twinges and he would quietly go to the bathroom on his own.

Gary went back to school almost immediately after he came home from the hospital. His sixth birthday was coming up on February 8, and he now was in the first grade.

Gary

It's funny, but the other kids didn't even know I was gone. The transplant and everything was done over the Christmas vacation, so they must've thought I was just a little late getting back because Mom and Dad took me somewhere, like to visit Grandma and Grandpa and Grandma-by-the-railroad down in Lima.

Mom and Dad and Dr. Firlit and Toni Greenslade all had explained to me that I was going to be small because of the kidney stuff. They kept telling me that size isn't as important as what a person has in his head and in his heart. Anyway, I worried for a while, but when I got back to school, I noticed that I still wasn't much smaller than the other kids in the first grade. I was maybe three-feet-four and they were maybe a couple of inches taller. There even were some girls who were shorter than me. So none of the kids teased me about my size. That came later.

I know that Mom told Mr. Fink, the principal, about my growth problem and maybe that's why he put me in Mrs. McGarrahan's class. Mrs. McGarrahan is what you call a "little person." She's not even four feet tall. She's married to Chuck McGarrahan. He's not even four feet tall, too, and he owns the Nu-Glow Cleaners in Zion. Mr. and Mrs. McGarrahan are very active in what she says is a national association of little people.

Mrs. McGarrahan is a very nice lady. She's very

smart, too. She kept talking all the time about how it doesn't matter how big or little you are, or what the color of your skin is, or if you're handicapped. There was one very tall kid in school and she kept telling him to stop thinking he was a freak.

Mrs. McGarrahan was very nice to me. I was ahead of the other kids in reading, and sometimes I'd get kind of bored and restless. When I did, Mrs. McGarrahan would say to me, "Now Gary, I want you to take this book and go down the hall and read out loud to the kids in the other classes." I guess the teachers in those classes knew she was going to do this because they always let me come in and read out loud.

One day Mom almost fell over when we were in the drugstore and we heard a big kid from the sixth grade say to his mom, "Hey, there's that little kid from the first grade who reads better than us."

Robert Fink, the principal, confirms Gary's early reading abilities. He also reports that the child hand-lettered and illustrated a four-page "newspaper," whose theme was the inadvisability of hitting other kids with snowballs in the schoolyard and playground. Fink was so impressed with this project —spelling errors and all—that he still keeps a photocopy for all doubting visitors to see.

It is one of Fink's policies to teach young children to play chess, as a learning tool. Chess apparently came easily to Gary. Both Willie and Grandfather Jack Lovelace remember playing the game with him when he was only six. "Gary never beat me, but he sure did know how to move the pieces around," Mr. Lovelace says, chuckling. "He never once mixed up a knight with a bishop."

Is there any correlation between Gary's kidney disease and his intelligence? Dr. Lewy thinks so. That's why he keeps IQ records on his young patients. "There's no explanation for it scientifically, he says, but there seems to be a compensation factor in mental prowess for children who have undergone kidney transplants. The bright ones become brighter; the dull ones have literally blossomed mentally after the early treatment and the transplant itself. It's not a panacea, of course. Some children have an instrinsic brain problem apart from the kidney malfunction, or even because of it, if it has not been detected for a long time. But on the whole, the correlation between intelligence and kidney therapy seems to us to be a phenomenon worth looking into."

The National Kidney Foundation's Dr. Ira Greifer is not so sure. He says, "Here, at Albert Einstein Medical Center, we have kids who come in dumb and when they leave, they're still dumb. With Gary, I'm sure he would have been bright, no matter what happened to him. So I don't think it's a compensation. I think it's a matter of these children spending so much time in hospitals, surrounded by extremely intelligent adults—doctors, nurses, interns, residents—who care about them and spend an inordinate amount of time with them. These people motivate the children to learn. Thus we have ghetto kids who go back to school in their neighborhoods and are far ahead of their classmates, because of all the reading and talking they've done in the hospital. The input they get here also makes a lot of kids want to go to college. They consider that it's expected of them by our group. So we have our transplant kids in top colleges like Columbia and UCLA. We even have one at the Yale Law School. I think the main reason for that is the intellectual stimulation they receive here."

Whichever theory one accepts, Gary, way down the ladder at first-grade level, was incontrovertibly doing extremely well. One of the most interesting signs of his advanced thinking was that he soon took over from his mother the tiresome task of constantly measuring the exact amount of fluids he drank and the exact amount of urine he excreted. One day he said, "Mom, I want to do it myself." Sue nervously acceded, and from that day on, there was the record, meticulously kept, and in millimeters, too. In those days, most six-year-olds didn't even know the metric system existed. Gary had learned it in the hospital—a nod in the direction of the Greifer Theory.

Once again, Willie marveled at his son and once again, perhaps coincidentally, took a series of moves to better himself.

Willie

I had had a tough time, during and after Gary's transplant. To make up for the work I missed going back and forth to the hospital, I was going to the lab at six-thirty in the morning instead of eight, and I was doing extra odd jobs in other departments at Abbott. For a little while, I was a nervous wreck, coming home and yelling at Sue, maybe just because she didn't have supper ready on time. Then I caught hold of myself, saying that if the good Lord spared Gary and made him so smart, I had no right to repay Him by doing like I was doing.

So, instead, I began to look around to see exactly where I could move up in the company. One day, on my rounds to the warehouse to pick up some chemicals for the lab, I found out that there was a good paying job coming up—Incoming Inspector. There were three Incoming Inspectors in the warehouse, and one was leaving. It was a job that called for a lot of skill. You had to know something about chemistry.

From my work in the lab, I already knew some of the rudiments. I certainly could tell sulfuric acid from sodium sulfate, for instance. But I had to know more. The only way to do that was to go back to school again at night. I took courses right there in the plant and courses on the outside. It was basic stuff, but I got to know organic and inorganic.

I went to see Dr. Gene Burgess, the department manager at Incoming Inspection, and applied for the job. I told him I would continue to take the courses. He said, "Well, you don't need to have a bachelor's degree. Let me just call Dr. Woroch over at the lab and find out what he says about you." I guess Dr. Woroch talked about me pretty good because I got the job.

I couldn't wait to tell Sue and Gary. I was going to get more money and more respect. It was pretty responsible work. Every chemical they use in Abbott must first pass through Incoming Inspection, and the inspector has to check and OK every bit of it.

This is what I still do at Abbott, and believe me, I recognized from the first day on the job that I now had come a long, long way from Housekeeping.

Willie's immediate supervisor is a handsome, bearded Nordic type named Skip Randle, who has known Willie since his earliest days at Abbott. He was among the friends in the company who suffered with Willie through all Gary's medical traumas.

Randle says, "Willie is very capable at what he does, and what he does is very important. He's only one of three men here who are responsible for that very crucial first assessment of all the chemicals that arrive here and eventually end up as the final product manufactured by the company for doctors, hospitals, pharmacies and labs. These men have to use their senses—sight, smell and touch—to make sure each raw chemical is what the label says it is, and that it isn't spoiled. There's back up, sure. Everything also gets tested and assayed by chemists, but a lot of goofs are caught by the three Incoming Inspectors before the errors can snowball."

Sue

I was so proud of Willie when he first got this job,

and the extra money sure did give us some peace of mind. Before that, we were mainly living on my salary, while most of Willie's salary was still going to paying off our old debts. It took him eight years to pay everything off through the budget plan set up by the company. Now we could breathe easier financially.

One thing I did *not* breathe easy about; I couldn't get it out of my mind what the doctors had said, after the transplant, about the probability that Gary would always be small. The most anyone would guess at was that he might reach four-feet-ten or five feet, but they weren't even sure of that. My worry was a continuation of what had been going through my mind for four years.

It went back to the first operation, the time when we knew he had a very severe problem and was going to have that problem for the rest of his life. The questions that kept running through my head were: How to deal with him growing up? How to prepare him and myself for the times he'd come to me and say, "Mommy, I want to play football. Why can't I play?"

So I'd think about that and I'd say to myself, "There's got to be something that he can do, that I can encourage him to do, that's going to be an outlet for him. It might be music or art or writing, or anything he could do and do well, so when the other kids were playing football or basketball and he had to be left out, at least he could say, "I can't do these physical things like you can, but there is something else *I* can do better."

I knew there still would be times when he'd say to me, "I want to play football," or "I want to play hockey," and I'd have to say, "You can't,"

A GIFT OF LIFE

and he might be depressed about it. After all, he's a boy and he has friends and there would be a lot of things he couldn't do as well, or at all. So basically it was a matter of how he was going to live with his problems as he got older.

We all knew he was a bright child. My mother, more than anyone else, was taken with this and she used to say she was sometimes frightened at what he'd say and what he'd do. She was the one who gave me the clue. She kept reminding me that Gary always was the family entertainer. Whatever was going on, he was the center of attention, mimicking people in a very funny and not-cruel, way, and using his imagination to make up funny little stories that somehow had a beginning, a middle and an end. Grandpa was his favorite target. He'd laugh at almost everything Gary said, so he'd just put on a little show for Grandpa. He'd turn flips, do acrobatics, take pratfalls—anything to make Grandpa laugh.

My mother kept mentioning all this to me. She also kept talking about all the funny little stories Gary kept writing in school, where Mrs. McGarrahan and the other teachers kept encouraging him to be creative. Finally I had an inspiration. Certainly a six-year-old child couldn't get far enough as a writer to make himself feel as important as the good football players in school. But a six-year-old child *might* be able to get up on a stage and make some sort of a name for himself in show business.

But what did I know about show business? I was still a country girl from Alabama with only a few years in north Chicago, Waukegan and Zion, Illinois. These were hardly centers of drama and entertainment. The most exciting thing we had in town was the fashion shows at Montgomery Ward.

And that was the very thought which gave me my notion. One of my little cousins, a twelve-year-old girl named Renée, was modeling in Montgomery Ward back-to-school fashion shows and such, and her mother told me that some of the kids in the shows had gone on to get work with modeling agencies in Chicago. I thought to myself, "So maybe this is the way you get started in show business in Zion, Illinois."

But then something came along to put all these thoughts out of my mind for the time being.

It was another phone call from Dr. Firlit. Gary had been doing so well in his checkups at the hospital that I'd forgotten there was another crisis point for rejection of a kidney at the six-month mark after the transplant operation.

The six months were just about up.

Dr. Firlit told me to bring Gary in and be prepared for him to stay for a few days. I had so much confidence in Gary's doctors by now that I didn't worry at all. I just figured this was going to be another, longer checkup and that they simply were going to do more complicated tests like a kidney scan and an ultrasound examination.

14

But the *doctors* were worried.

Gary's previous blood chemistries had showed a gradually increasing rise in the creatinine level (meaning that the function of the new kidney had lessened to the extent that it was leaking some waste products into the blood). Before that, Gary's creatinine had risen but with the adjustment of drug dosages, had once again fallen back within normal levels. Also the white blood cell count was high, an indication that the lymphocytes were mobilizing more antibodies in the war to destroy the "foreign invader" they considered Gary's new kidney to be.

In short, all symptoms pointed to the distressing fact that Gary might be having an acute rejection episode which, if untreated, could possibly result in his losing the kidney.

Two days of further tests at Children's Memorial convinced Dr. Lewy and Dr. Firlit that significant counterrejection action had to be taken. They decided on radiation of the kidney. In this procedure, the kidney area is bombarded with X-rays or a concentrated beam of gamma rays from radioactive isotopes. The idea is to kill off as many white cells as possible to lessen the intensity of their attack on the new kidney's tissue. Radiation was used much more in 1974 than it is today. Now, the most common counterrejection methods are to remove lymph tissue or to inject substances like ALG (anti-lymphocyte globulin), in order to halt or slow down the increasing attack of the white cells. Some practitioners still successfully use radiation, but most fear a possible side effect to the kidney called radiation nephritis. The amazing increase of knowledge in the field of nephrology over the last few years has spurred a preference for the newer, more sophisticated techniques.

In 1974, however, radiation was still the method of choice at Children's Memorial. So Gary was taken to the radiation room and covered with a lead apron which exposed only the kidney area in its artificially created pocket down in his lower left abdomen.

The radiation was turned on and the ray particles bombarded the pocket for just a few brief seconds. Gary felt nothing. He was returned to his bed and resumed playing with his toys.

Willie and Sue felt nothing, either. The procedure was so simple compared with what had gone on before that they suffered no anxiety. They had signed the consent papers for the radiation, but as Sue said, "As long as our boy was in that hospital, we felt that nothing bad could happen to him."

Happily, their abiding trust was not misplaced. Within hours after the radiation, Gary's creatinine and white blood cell levels began to drop. To aid the process permanently, new immunosuppressive drugs were added to the daily dosages of those he already was taking. Two days later, Dr. Lewy was sure that the rejection had indeed been reversed and that the kidney was stable, with no radiation side effects. He admits he heaved a sigh of relief before he told Sue she could take Gary home, but that she now had two extra pills to give him every day.

So the Colemans went back to Zion, with Gary returning to school and Willie and Sue to their jobs.

Unflappable Sue. She almost immediately resumed work on her project to get Gary into show business or some other area in which he could excel, as compensation for the physical things he might not be able to do because of his projected small stature.

Sue

I spoke to my cousin whose daughter, Renée, was doing the fashion shows at Montgomery Ward and I asked her if they used little boys in the shows as well as little girls. She didn't know, but she said, "Why don't you write to them?"

Before I did that, I figured I'd better check the idea out with Gary. Even then, when he was only six-and-a-half, we always made a point of getting his input on anything that concerned him. I had him listen to Renée talk about the fashion shows and I said to him, "Would you like to do that?"

He said, "I think I would. I could do that."

I said, "But I'm not even sure they take little boys." He came up with the same idea as my cousin but took it one step further. He said, "Why don't *I* write them a letter and find out?" I thought it was a marvelous notion for him to write the letter instead of me, so I told him to sit down and do it. He wrote the letter, and I said to myself I'd mail it and if we didn't hear anything, at least he'd be satisfied that he wrote the letter and tried.

But they did respond to it, saying, "Yes, we think it would be a good idea to add little boys to our fashion shows." It was June and they were already planning their back-to-school show for August. Gary was very blasé about it, but I was amazed and terribly excited.

Sue still has photocopies of that historic correspondence between Gary and the Waukegan store of Montgomery Ward. Printed in his childish hand, Gary's letter reads as follows: "Do you use little boys? I am six years old. I am in the first grade. I am thoroughly well-mannered and people tell me I look like Rodney Allen Rippey." The letter concludes with "Sincerely yours" and is signed Gary Wayne Coleman.

For the uninitiated, Rodney Allen Rippey is another fetching black child, who at the age of three and a half enchanted the West Coast and the Midwest in TV commercials for the Jack-in-the-Box fast-food chain in the early 1970s.

A GIFT OF LIFE

Sue

The time came for the Montgomery Ward fashion show and I was a basket case. I thought, "Well, it's one thing when you're entertaining the family and close friends, but when you walk out in front of an audience, that's a whole different ball game." But I was really interested in seeing what his reaction would be, so I decided we should go through with it, for that reason alone.

On the day of the show we went to the store, along with a lot of relatives who all brought cameras to take pictures of Gary's part in the event. That made me even more nervous.

The Montgomery Ward people gave Gary a little three-piece blue corduroy suit to wear. He not only had to put on a vest but also a shirt and tie. He wasn't used to that kind of formal clothing, so he fussed and fidgeted a lot.

Then they briefed us on what Gary was supposed to do. There was a narrator, and when she said, "Now we'll have a look at what Montgomery Ward is featuring this year for little boys," that was Gary's cue. He was supposed to walk out on the stage, turn around twice and then walk off, as dignified as possible. He did it a couple of times in rehearsal and was OK.

The show began. While the little girls did their thing, Gary was running around backstage, having a lot of fun with the props and with Linda Secor, who was a regular in the shows and later got to produce them. By the time the narrator came up with Gary's cue, I guess he forgot what he was supposed to do.

Gary

I was foolin' around with Linda backstage when someone yelled, "Come on, Gary, you're on." I ran out and saw all those people. It threw me for a minute and I stumbled and tripped over my own feet. Then I was supposed to spin around two times to show the people the suit I was wearing, but I forgot how many turns they wanted me to do, so I made it four spins, just to be sure. That made me dizzy and I stumbled again. This time I fell down.

By now I was so nervous that I ran off the stage, in the wrong direction. Linda yelled, "Go back. Go back. You've still got to do that bit with Amy." So I ran back, and Amy was parading around in a blue coat. My job was to be the perfect gentleman and help her off with the coat so she could show the people the dress she had on underneath. I think the dress was kind of plaid.

I got ahold of Amy's coat by the collar, like they told me, and I tried to slip it off. The coat stuck and it wouldn't move. It was too small, I guess, and Amy was a little too fat. I kept yanking on the coat and Amy kept squirming around, trying to help me. It must've looked like some kind of crazy dance as we tried to get that dumb coat off.

Finally, Amy came loose from the coat all of a sudden and she nearly fell down. I was so danged mad by that time that I just threw the coat down on the stage and walk off. It was the wrong side of the stage again and Linda had to send me back. Everybody was laughing.

Sue

I watched and heard all this and covered my eyes with embarrassment. I said to myself, "Good Lord, he's blown it."

Afterwards I was thinking, "Well, this wasn't important anyway," when the store manager, a Mr. Glenn Hoffman, came over to talk to me. He said, "Your son was terrific. He gave us a laugh just when we needed it. He's so *cute*. Could we use him again in future shows?"

"Sure," I said weakly.

15

Gary did another Montgomery Ward fashion show early in December 1974, modeling a boy's snowsuit for Christmas. This time there was no attempt to coach him. They just let him use his own free-wheeling style and he once again got an enormous response from the crowd.

All in all, it was an exciting Christmas season for Gary. December 18 was the first anniversary of his transplant operation, and Willie and Sue, not wanting him to think back on it traumatically, decided to convert the anniversary into a festive occasion. They said to Gary, "Next Thursday is the kidney's birthday. We're going to have a party and everyone will bring you presents to help the kidney celebrate. Do you realize what a lucky kid you are? Most other kids only get presents once at this time of the year. You're going to get them twice—on the kidney's birthday and on Christmas Day."

A GIFT OF LIFE

Gary

When Mom told me that, I thought it was a great idea, especially the part about my getting another set of presents so close to Christmas. Only I couldn't figure out what the party would be like. Remember, I was only six years old then, and the only parties I ever had before was with a lot of kids, mostly my cousins, and we wore funny hats and ate ice cream and cookies and drank a lot of pop. It was always in the afternoon and there was a lot of decorations hanging up. I wondered what kind of decorations you put up when a kidney is having a birthday. I said dumb things like maybe we should hang up pictures of kidneys with funny hats on them, and Mom got mad and said I was saying dumb things.

Anyway, it wasn't like any of the other parties at all. Mom put up a few streamers and the guests were all grown-ups. We didn't start until about six o'clock because it was a Wednesday and the grown-ups had to wait until it was after work. There was Carl and Bruce and Mary Ann and Judy, and they all were from Abbott, where Dad works. Mom told me in advance that they were the folks who stood by us best when I was sick and had the transplant. She also said that Carl and Mary Ann and Bruce were big scientists and that some of them were doctors, and that I should be sure to behave.

Well, they all came in, and everybody congratulated my kidney, and they gave me presents.

Mom and Dad gave me a couple of presents, too. I remember that one of them was a dynamite model of a Santa Fe caboose, which I still have. Then we sat down to eat and I remember Mom saying something like they also were celebrating that she now had her head above water and didn't feel like she was drowning any more. Everybody drank to that with champagne and they even let me have a little sip. Carl said that was so it could go down to my kidney and it would know it was a special day and a celebration. I thought that was funny and I laughed a lot.

I really liked Carl and Mary Ann, and one of the best things that came out of the party was when Mom told me a few weeks later that after the party at our house, they decided to get married.

All in all, the kidney's first birthday was a rousing success, and Gary never once seemed troubled by thoughts of the fearsome events of a year earlier. In fact, the stratagem worked so well on Gary emotionally, and also on Sue and Willie, that they still celebrate the kidney's birthday with a party and gifts every year on December 18.

The most joyous kidney's birthday party of all came in 1975. That was the end of the second year since the transplant, the cut-off point after which nephrologists believe that the possibility of acute rejection of the kidney by the body is almost negligible. All of Gary's tests at Children's Memorial confirmed that indeed the transplant was doing extremely well. The kidney function never was perfect, and there were ups and downs in the organ's performance, but adjustments in the drug dosages always kept it within acceptable limits.

Also, there had been several kidney scans, in which Gary swallowed a medication which allowed the kidney to be minutely examined by X-ray devices. The scans all indicated that while there was some damage to the tissue in the rejection episode of June 1974, more than enough of the million nephrons were operating efficiently to allow him to continue to lead a normal life, with the exception of the mandatory medications and hospital checkups.

So the kidney's birthday party on December 18, 1975, was an uproarious affair, with grandparents, uncles, aunts and cousins present.

There was something else to celebrate, too.

A few months earlier, Sue had been approached by Glenn Hoffman, who had become the head of all the Montgomery Ward stores in the area. By now, Gary had done several of the fashion shows at the Waukegan store and Sue was getting discouraged. Nothing else seemed to be happening and she had no idea of where to go from there. Hoffman solved the problem for her. He said, "Your son has a lot of natural talent and I think he'd do very well getting modeling jobs down in Chicago. Why don't you call this friend of mine?" Hoffman gave her the telephone number and address of the A-Plus Talent Agency in Chicago.

Sue had called the agency, only to learn that Hoffman's friend no longer was there. But they said, "Bring your little boy in anyway, with some snapshots. We register children on Thursdays."

Sue

I took Gary down to A-Plus the following Thursday. Gary caused a lot of excitement when we walked in. Rodney Allen Rippey, of the Jack-in-the-Box TV commercials, was still fresh in everybody's mind, and they said, "My God, this kid may be *another* one." There were definite similarities. Both were short, chubby, bright, very cute little boys. The agency people talked about that for a while and I got a little annoyed. Like any mother, I thought my son was too special to be compared with anyone.

In the meantime, I didn't think Gary was helping himself any. He was running around the office, examining gadgets on people's desks, playing with the secretaries' typewriters. I considered that he was being a pest and I told him so, but they all kept saying, "Isn't he the cutest little thing?"

Anyway, they registered Gary and I got him out of there. I had no idea of what was going to happen next. When nothing did happen over the next few weeks, I once again began to think of other things, like music, as an outlet for Gary. I began to look around for someone to give him piano lessons.

Then, out of the blue, I got a call from A-Plus. They had a spot for Gary in a McDonald's hamburger commercial for television. Was I interested? I was so excited that I said, "Of course," without even asking when or where or how much.

A GIFT OF LIFE

Gary was pretty matter-of-fact, except that he began practicing funny faces in the mirror. At six-and-a-half, I guess, there doesn't seem to be much difference between a local fashion show and a TV commercial that was going to be seen nationally. He was cool; I was frantic.

When I got him down to the studio in Chicago, there wasn't much to be frantic about. There was the usual mob scene of kids used by McDonald's in their commercials. All Gary had to do was a brief shot of a little boy trying to play with a basketball that was too big for him. I didn't think it was much, but apparently the McDonald's advertising agency people did. A few days later, they called A-Plus for Gary to appear in their Valentine's Day commercial.

So when we had Gary's kidney's second birthday party, we had something else to celebrate, too: Gary's first TV appearances at forty dollars an hour.

Actually they weren't his first on television. After his transplant, Dr. Firlit had had Gary on a local ABC show with him. Dr. Firlit was discussing the new advances in nephrology, and with Gary squirming around in his arms, he had said, "Would you believe that this young man had a kidney transplant just six weeks ago?"

By 1976, then, Gary's medical condition was stable and something resembling a career was beginning to bud. In one other crucial area, however, he was doing badly. It was the one aspect of his illness that Sue always had dreaded and whose impact she so wisely was trying to combat. At school, the other children in his class were spurting in size and Gary wasn't. By the third grade, some of the boys were a head taller.

And Gary wasn't handling it very well.

Robert Fink, the principal of Gary's school, was the first to notice it. A dedicated fortyish man from a rural area of Illinois, Fink had completed his twenty-first year in education, including three years in an Air Force school in Japan, and his basic philosophy is: "The children with needs are the most rewarding to me; the little steps seem so big when they take them." A white man who strongly advocates integrated learning, he had most of the children of Zion's twenty-percent black population in his Shiloh Park school.

On day, Fink looked out his office window toward the playground and saw Gary being picked up and tossed around by the bigger children. "At first, Gary seemed to be going along with it and was having fun," Fink says, "but then I could see that he wanted to stop but the others didn't. Gary started to throw punches. He hit pretty hard for a little guy. I saw a teacher break up the scuffle and I just filed the incident away in the back of my mind. But then, it happened again—and again. Gary was brought to my office for disciplinary purposes. I sat him down and we had a long talk about how he could cope with his smallness. I told him he was a very personable young man who liked to play, but that he should never incite the other kids into anything that might turn out to be rough stuff. I told him that if they teased him about being small, to use his capacity to make them laugh by teasing back, good-humoredly. I told him to come into my office to talk it out with me, whenever things started to get out of hand."

Unfortunately, things kept getting out of hand,

with Gary still throwing punches, and the boy spent a lot of time in the principal's office. Fink says, "I think I finally won him over by steering him into gaining the other kids' respect, and distracting them from his size, by doing the things he did best. What he did best was reading and writing. The teachers and I got him to write his little short stories and read them to his own class and to the other classes. He even involved the other kids in acting them out. He really was the best pupil I ever had in his ability to express himself. So I further encouraged him to continue writing his newspapers, which the others enjoyed. I particularly remember one issue, in which he editorialized: 'Mr. Fink is a gentle man, but if something is wrong, he simply has to stop or do. Mr. Fink's command is: bloody noses mean trouble. That is Mr. Fink's command. Question: If Mr. Fink expels someone, does that mean better or worse? More on Page Four.' And he went on. I still have that hand-printed newspaper.

"In any event," Fink continues, "when Gary won the other kids' respect with his brightness, they began to leave him alone. Then, when he became a celebrity whom they could see in TV commercials, the teasing about his size stopped completely."

Sue Coleman thinks that Fink is being overly modest about his influence on Gary in her son's struggle for self-esteem.

Sue

Mr. Fink was remarkable with Gary. In his way, he was doing the same thing I was trying to do with the modeling career, and the two approaches meshed perfectly. We were both teaching Gary that there were things he could do better, even though he couldn't keep up with the other kids physically. Except for punching, unfortunately. By reducing his aggression against the kids who were teasing him, Mr. Fink may have even gotten Gary off the road to delinquency.

It was terrible in the beginning. Not only did the boys tease him and toss him around, but the little girls wanted to pick Gary up and play with him, like he was a doll. I remember Gary telling me how nearly every day, he'd go to Mr. Fink's office and they'd sit there and talk it out. Sometimes he went there on his own; sometimes Mr. Fink had to go out into the playground to rescue him and bring him in. Gary told me how Mr. Fink would say things like, "If a tall boy calls you 'midget' or 'shrimpo,' just laugh it off, ha, ha, ha, and say something like, 'How's your head doing up there in the stratosphere, daddy-long-legs?'"

And eventually, Gary *did* win the other kids over by being smart, by doing the newspaper and his little stories, and by making up word games he could play better than anyone else.

All in all, I think that next to Willie and me, Mr. Fink had more of an influence on his growing-up

A GIFT OF LIFE

years than almost anyone else. He was with Gary for three years, and after Gary was transferred to East Elementary School, he again was his principal for three more years. It probably isn't true, but I always had the feeling that Mr. Fink got himself transferred to East so he could continue to be with Gary.

At Shiloh Park, the time hadn't come yet, but Mr. Fink was instilling in Gary the same philosophy we were trying to plant in his head, and it eventually took hold. The philosophy was: "I can accept the way I am."

Willie has his own, more macho version of the events that took place in Gary's travail at Shiloh Park School.

Willie

What happened was this: There was these two big kids, one white and one black, who was the roughest on Gary. The white kid and the black kid were friends. One day, Gary just hauled off and popped this white kid right on the jaw. He could hardly reach his jaw, except when the kid was bending over, but he managed to pop him good and he knocked the kid right on his ass. He also gave him a black eye, before he was dragged off to Mr. Fink's office.

When Sue got to school to bring Gary home

that day, the kid's mother came over and said, "Look what your son did to my son. He gave him a black eye." Sue almost fit to died with laughing. She said, "You mean to tell me my little son did that to your big son?" The woman looked down at Gary and was embarrassed and went away.

That was the turning point for Gary. After that, these two big kids, the white one and the black one, became his best friends. He used to bring them home to play with his trains after school. I used to see the blond one around there a lot.

And the way it was, these two big kids became Gary's protectors. They said, "Anyone lays a hand on Gary, or bad-mouths him, they got to deal with us."

With Gary himself as a not-too-reliable source, given his imagination, the truth is probably an amalgam of all the various versions. It soon became academic, however, as Gary's out-of-school career metamorphosed from bud to blossom.

16

The two McDonald's commercials led to a Valentine's Day TV commercial for Hallmark greeting cards. In the filming, Gary, while fooling around between takes, decided to paste a Valentine card on his head. "Let's shoot that," the director said, cracking up. And that's the way the commercial eventually ran on the air, with the card stuck firmly to Gary's forehead above his round little beaming brown face.

If nothing else, this antic performance attracted a lot of attention in the Chicago advertising community. It seemed to open the gates. Sue got a lot of calls to bring Gary into Chicago after school or on weekends. He became one of the favorites of the advertising agencies for what is called "demo commercials"—sample commercials to persuade an advertiser to embark on a concept for a certain kind of television advertising campaign. At the same time, since his voice was now discovered to be as fetching as his face, he also did a lot of radio commercials and television "voice-overs" in which he was heard but not seen.

Then came a "print" phase in which he was seen but not heard—in newspaper ads and merchandise catalogues. His cheerful face kept popping up, particularly in ads for the World Book Encyclopedia and in the pages of the catalogue of the huge Spiegel mail-order house. He was photographed in the act of reading, playing, dressing, walking, running, reclining and committing all the tomfoolery that a normal seven-year-old boy is capable of committing.

Sue

He was seven by that time. It was late in 1975. Our lives had completely turned around. Gary was making pretty good money, Willie was making better money, and I was still at my job at Victory Memorial. Our financial worries were finally a thing of the past.

But it was a pretty complicated existence we were living now. I had to go to work, make sure that Gary took all his medications, make sure he got to and from school on time, make sure he got to Chicago for his hospital checkups and for his photo and TV sessions. Willie and I spelled each other in these duties whenever possible. It wasn't easy.

A GIFT OF LIFE

But then there was a breakthrough that started a series of events which made Willie and me keep looking at one another and saying, "Can you *believe* what's happening?"

With all his exposure, Gary still wasn't anything special. There were a lot of kids running around Chicago doing commercials and "print" photography. So I didn't think too much of it when the ad agency for the Harris Trust and Savings Bank called in a lot of kids for a TV commercial they had in mind. It was another "cattle call," which usually isn't very pleasant. They call a lot of kids in and look them over like a bunch of calves while they make their choices. Gary was one of six children picked, but it didn't look too promising. I figured he'd just be part of a bunch of kids running around on camera.

It didn't turn out that way.

The Harris Bank has a mascot which they have always used in their commercials. The mascot is a fuzzy little toy lion, called the Hubert Doll. Every August and September, they run a TV campaign to bring children into the bank to open savings accounts, and for depositing a certain amount, a kid gets a Hubert Doll free. Before this, they usually used an animated Hubert Doll on camera, with adult voices telling how you could get yours. This year they decided to focus on children.

So we went down to the studio and they had a script worked out with a lot of children milling around and doing things, but after a while, I noticed the director and producers were focusing on Gary. It ended up with him as kind of the star. After you saw all the other children, the commercial wound up with little Gary sitting in a big chair, reading to his Hubert Doll.

The commercial went on the air and everyone loved it. The kids in Gary's school stopped bugging him about his size; now they were bugging him about wanting to take his picture. The Harris Bank people told Willie and me that they had got a lot of mail and a lot of deposits out of the commercial, and they asked if Gary would be the spokesman for the bank in the 1976 campaign.

We said sure, and we brought Gary in to make the first of another batch of commercials. This is what really made Gary famous in Chicago and started all the good things that have happened to him since.

Gary

When Mom got the call about the new Harris Bank commercial, I was out in the backyard playin' with my dog, Champion. I didn't get too excited. In fact, there isn't very much to get excited about in making *any* commercials. I learned that when I did my first one for McDonald's. I got myself all pumped up and we went to a McDonald's highway restaurant way out in the middle of nowhere. Soon I wasn't pumped up anymore because it was so boring. For three hours Mom and I had to stand around while the crew set up the cameras and the lights. Then they called in

A GIFT OF LIFE   137

each kid, one at a time, while the rest of us stood around some more. When it came to be my turn, I had to walk up to the counter and order a hamburger. They shot that over and over again, about twenty times. Then they called in the next kid and Mom and I went home. Big deal.

I thought it would be the same thing with the new Harris Bank commercial. It started out that way, but boy, was I wrong.

Dad drove us to a house in Evanston and said he'd come back and pick us up again after he finished work. We got there about eight-thirty in the morning, and as usual, Mom and I stood around for about six hours while the crew set up inside the house. There were about forty people in the crew for that one bitty commercial. They moved furniture and set up their lights and sound equipment. It was real boring for me because I was the only person in this commercial, so there weren't even any other kids for me to fool around with.

Finally, at about two-thirty in the afternoon, the director came over and told me my lines. He said that the commercial was to be done in two scenes. In the first, I had to be walking up a flight of stairs in the house, carrying a Hubert Doll, and telling how I just got the Hubert Doll at the Harris Bank because I opened a savings account there. I should've figured something tricky was coming up because the director wouldn't give me my lines for the second scene. He said, "All you have to do is open a closet door. Then I'll tell you what to say."

So I went in and I did the first scene, walking up the steps, time after time after time. Then the director said we'd do the second scene. We went to a closet in the upstairs hall of the house. The cameras and the lights were all set up already. The director said, "OK, Gary, open the closet door." I opened the door and a whole waterfall of Hubert Dolls came tumbling down on my head. There must've been *thirty* of them. They all wear little plastic eyeglasses and they hurt when they hit me. I heard the director say, "Keep that camera going on his face. It's just the look I want. That's why I didn't tell the kid."

The dolls had knocked me to the floor and I was sitting there, up to my eyes in Huberts. The director came over and said, "That was perfect, Gary. If you had known what was coming it wouldn't have been anywhere near as good. Now, here's the line you're supposed to say while you're sitting there in the middle of all those dolls: 'Well, you can't have *enough* Hubert Dolls.' "

So I said the line, over and over again, and they kept shooting the dolls falling out of the closet over and over again, but at least they didn't have to fall on *me* again because the director kept saying he could never top that first shot of the look on my face when I didn't know what was coming. Finally Dad came for us when it was already dark outside and we went home.

Sue

When this commercial went on the air, Gary suddenly became famous all through the Chicago area. Wherever we went, people would say, "Oh, there's that cute little boy with the Hubert Dolls." The bank even began to have Gary make personal appearances. I'll never forget one of them. It was a banquet at the Palmer House, one of Chicago's biggest hotels. They sent a limousine all the way to Zion to fetch Willie and Gary and me. When we got to the banquet room in the hotel, there was a huge six-foot Hubert Doll lion up on the dais. But Gary was the surprise guest and Willie had to keep him hidden in the men's room until they were ready to call him onto the dais.

There were a lot of speeches and then Gary was introduced. Everybody cheered and he came out and stood near the giant Hubert Doll and he had to make a little speech. Then he mingled with the people down on the floor and he signed autographs. It was a very nice affair.

When it was time to go home, we got into the limousine and there was the six-foot lion sitting in the back. It was a gift for Gary, which he still keeps in his playroom at home. That ride up the expressway was one of the wildest I've ever had. People would pass us in their cars and they'd see the giant lion just riding along in the back seat. Their eyes would pop. Then they'd fall back and pull alongside again, to make sure they weren't hallucinating or something. Gary missed all this. He had fallen asleep with his head on the giant Hubert Doll's lap.

Another time, there was something called Executive's Day at the bank. Gary was the star attraction. He was dressed in a three-piece dark suit with a tie so that he looked just like one of the bank's vice presidents. And that's what he was for the day. People came swarming in and he would greet them and talk to them like it was *his* bank. After they made a deposit, he'd stamp their deposit slip with a Hubert Stamp, which then would qualify them to go over and receive their Hubert Doll. That little stunt even made the TV nightly news in Chicago.

Willie and Sue were unaware that Gary's Hubert Doll celebrity was extending well beyond Chicago. A thousand miles away in New York and two thousand miles away in Hollywood, moves were being made in TV executive suites to "Try to do something about that cute little black kid in Chicago in the commercials where the little lion dolls fall on his head out of the closet."

Television really is a very small industry, and word gets around fast.

17

One of the executives involved in the moves to nab Gary Coleman was Fred Silverman, then the head of programming at ABC (he had not yet moved over to become president of rival network, NBC).

Regarding his initial interest in Gary for ABC in 1976, Silverman says, "The problem was that I didn't move fast enough. The commercial with Gary and the lion dolls won a Clio as one of the best commercials of the year. The local ABC station used Gary as a guest on *AM-Chicago* with film clips from the commercial. This had to be fed to ABC in New York to be cleared. Someone in ABC-New York made a cassette of the tape and sent it to me with a note, saying 'Take a look at *this* kid.' I was busy and I didn't get around to looking at the cassette for some time. When I did, I told our people, '*Sign* that kid.' I was a few days too late. Norman Lear had already signed Gary for his Tandem Productions."

Norman Lear is the founding father and proprietor of such landmark TV series as *All in the Family, Maude, Sanford and Son* and *Mary Hartman, Mary Hartman.* Lear says, "What happened in the matter of little Gary Coleman in 1976 was this: My partner, Jerry Perenchio, always had been in love with the Our Gang comedies when he was a kid. They later ran on television as *The Little Rascals*. Jerry wanted to do a modern version of *The Little Rascals* for syndication in TV. So he sent a casting director named Bob Morones around the country to try to find another batch of kids to be the new Little Rascals. The first thing I knew about all this was when young Mr. Coleman walked into my office in Hollywood with a cheap little camera one day, and *he* wanted to take *my* picture."

Some of the interim events in this bizarre sequence are filled in by Victor Perillo, who is Gary's very able agent to this day. While Gary was still concentrating on "print" ads, the A-Plus Agency in Chicago had acquired Perillo from New York, where he had been a successful theatrical agent. A-Plus wanted to move out of its strictly local advertising-oriented sphere to operate nationally in TV and films, and they thought Perillo was the man who could do it for them. He was—at least in the case of Gary Coleman.

Says Perillo, "I heard that Tandem was sending Bob Morones around the country looking for new Little Rascals, so I told a friend of mine in New York to make sure to impress on Morones that he ought to call me when he came through Chicago. My message to Morones was, 'Have I got a kid for you.' Well, Morones arrived and he looked at a lot of kids, and then he got around to calling me."

Sue Coleman picks up the story from there:

Sue

After the success of the Harris Bank commercial, Gary got a Bisquick commercial that was to be filmed in Los Angeles. We were all getting ready to make our first airplane trip and we had plenty to do. We had to arrange for a nephrologist at Children's Hospital in Los Angeles in case anything went wrong. We also had our hands full keeping Gary's excitement under control, so we didn't pay much attention when we heard that Tandem people were in town looking for kids to act in a new *Little Rascals* series. The way they were doing it was the way we hated. They were just holding a series of "cattle calls," so we decided to ignore it.

On the day we were leaving, we suddenly got a call from Vic Perillo. Vic said that the Tandem people wanted to see Gary alone, not at a cattle call, and could we stop off at their hotel on our way to the airport. We weren't too thrilled, but we said OK. We went by the hotel and they read with Gary. They said they were impressed with him. They said they already had one little black boy to play Buckwheat, but maybe they might add a second one, Stymie, who showed up after Buckwheat in the original Our Gang movie comedies. They suggested that as long as we were going to Los Angeles anyway, could we stop in and see the Tandem executives in Hollywood?

We went to the airport and got on the plane. Gary had a ball on the flight with all the stewardesses not being able to keep their hands off him. He has that effect on people. Aside from that, he was swamped with comic books and word games, which kept him occupied all the way to L.A.

When we arrived, we were put up at the Franklin Plaza Hotel by General Mills, for whom Gary was doing the Bisquick commercial. Gary shot the commercial the next day with Lillian Randolph, a very nice older lady who had been Madame Queen in the original *Amos 'n' Andy* series. Gary loved her. He said she reminded him of both of his grandmas.

We went back to the hotel when the commercial was finished and I called a telephone number the Tandem people had given me in Chicago. Within a half hour, they had sent a car to pick us up and take us to Metromedia, where Tandem has its offices and studios. While we were waiting, Gary saw Norman Lear come in. He recognized him with his little hat and all. Gary had his camera with him, so bold as brass, he just followed Mr. Lear into his office and asked him if he could take his picture. Mr. Lear closed the door and Gary was in there for quite a while. I didn't know what they were talking about.

• • •

A GIFT OF LIFE

Lear says: "So there I was with this darling little boy in my office, moving me around and taking pictures. I finally realized who he was. I closed the door and I said, 'Gary, let's improvise a scene.' This is a technique I use a lot with grown actors. I said, 'Let's suppose I'm your older brother, and you've saved and saved and bought me a tie for my birthday. Now I'm going out on a big night and you want to know why I'm not wearing the tie. We're going to talk and you're going to let me know how your feelings are really hurt.' We did the scene, making it up as we went along, and all I can say is that if the kid didn't make me cry, he brought me to a tear. As he first argued and then told me how he was hurt, *I* was hurt. Standing there with this little open face and wet eyes, my eyes got wet, too. In all the years I've been using this acting test, nobody, at any age, ever did it better. So I went to my door and said to the *Little Rascals* people waiting out there, 'Make sure we use this little fellow.' "

So the new role of Stymie was written into the scripts for Gary, resulting in two black children in the cast instead of one.

The Colemans went home to Zion, Vic Perillo negotiated a contract for Gary, and a few weeks later Sue and Gary were back in Hollywood for the start of filming. School was out then, so there was no interruption in Gary's educational process. Also, copies of Gary's medical records had been transferred to Children's Hospital in Los Angeles so he could have his regular monthly checkup there.

The filming went on for three and a half weeks, during which three episodes of *The Little Rascals* were filmed. But then, as often occurs in the entertainment business, nothing happened. The series couldn't be sold. As Lear explains it, "We made a mistake. We couldn't compete with the forty-year-old *Little Rascals* that were still running on television." Sue philosophizes, "Those children were unique and it's very hard to reproduce a Little Rascal, as hard as it would be to reproduce a Shirley Temple."

Gary was put under a "holding contract," by Tandem, however. None of the other children in the cast were so honored. A "holding contract" meant that for a small amount of money per month, Gary could not do a series for anyone else, with, it was hoped, Tandem eventually coming up with another concept in which he could star. Months went by, while Gary just kept going to school and getting his medical checkups.

Vic Perillo, however, was not inactive. Says Perillo, "Knowing Fred Silverman's initial interest in Gary, I took him to New York, along with Sue and Willie, to meet all the people at ABC. They were fascinated with Gary and came up with a lot of ideas for movies and specials. But then they'd always back off, saying, 'We're afraid of that Norman Lear contract he has with Tandem.' Finally I went back to Hollywood with the Colemans and I said to the Tandem people, 'You've got this kid under contract. You've got a lot of shows. At least give him a little exposure by letting him appear on them as a guest star.' They agreed. And Gary began appearing in *The Jeffersons, Good Times* and *America 2 Night*."

Norman Lear sees it from a different angle. Lear says, "Vic Perillo doesn't know this, but Fred Silverman who was still at ABC, called my partner, Bud

Yorkin, and said, 'I love this little boy and I want to do a show with him.' Yorkin relayed this information to me. I said, 'Bud, I think the kid has star potential, but I want him to get used to the lights and audiences, and I'd like to get to know his on-screen personality a little better. So why don't we use him in our shows and groom him for a little while. Our *Little Rascals* was on film, so who knows if the kid can even memorize lines for a half-hour taping.' Bud said, 'Fine.'

"Two days later, the phone rang and it was Fred Silverman. Without even saying hello, he hit me with, 'What do you mean we can't do something with Gary Coleman?' It was like I was robbing him. I told Fred what we had in mind in the way of *The Jeffersons* and our other shows, explaining that this was sort of a training period before he embarked on something more important. Fred hung up, furious.

"So much for the shrewd manipulations that go on behind the scenes in television's executive suites. But in any event, we immediately used Gary in two *Good Times* episodes. He was dynamite and the audience loved him. He could handle the camera and the lights and the timing. Everything about it was right. He even knew how to hold a pause for a second, waiting for the laugh from the audience. He was a natural, as if he had been doing stand-up comic routines for years, and I knew he'd never had a lesson."

Early in 1978, however, Lear withdrew from active daily participation in Tandem's operations, though he continued in his ownership position. The company now was being run by Al Burton and Alan Horn. Among the legacies acquired by Burton and Horn were just two contracts with actors. The first was the one with Gary Coleman. The second was with Conrad Bain, the urbane, middle-aged Canadian Scot who had been lured by Lear from a successful Broadway theater career to play the right-wing neighbor to the left-wing Bea Arthur in the Tandem series, *Maude*.

"*Oy vay*" is what Burton is reputed to have said to Horn.

18

The Colemans knew very little of what was going on in the executive-suite chess games, except for what they learned from Vic Perillo.

Sue

All that concerned me was that they were hauling Gary back and forth to Los Angeles. It was very disruptive to our lives and I was beginning to think I wasn't sure I liked show business. My hospital was very good about it. They didn't mind that I took off from work so often to go with Gary. The law required that I be with him. At school, Mr. Fink didn't mind because Gary only missed a few days of classes at a time, and by taking reading assignments with him, he was always able to keep up. Besides, a tutor is required by the State of California to be on every movie and television set where children are working. The tutors helped Gary with his assignments.

The biggest problem was that Willie had used up all his vacation time and couldn't make most of the trips. He was doing very well in his inspector's job at Abbott and was becoming kind of an indispensable man. But I missed him and he missed us. We talked on the phone a couple of times a day when I was on those short trips to L.A. with Gary.

When Gary was doing those guest shots on *The Jeffersons* and the other Tandem shows, I tried as much as possible not to be the typical stage mother. I stayed in the background and was only there when Gary needed me. Mostly, I had to keep a close eye on him to make sure he didn't nibble a lot of potato chips, corn chips, pretzels, peanuts—all the salty things that might cause fluids to accumulate in his body and bring on trouble with the kidney. Aside from that, I never interfered with what the director and the crew were doing. Some other mothers were hovering around their children like every camera angle was a make-or-break situation.

We lived in little motels and hotels near the studio and it wasn't a very pleasant life for Gary or for me. We'd be at the studio rehearsing or taping all day; at night we'd watch television until Gary fell asleep. I saw a lot of cartoons and old

Abbott and Costello movies. The one show we had in common was *60 Minutes*, which Gary has always loved. Mostly, I guess, I was edgy because while Gary was doing very well in the guest shots, nothing else seemed to be happening. Those were the times when Vic Perillo picked me up. He kept telling me, "It's going to *happen*. It's going to *happen*."

Then, in June 1978, he said, "It's *happening*." He said there was a series pilot script being prepared for ABC. I believed him when he said he'd better look around for entertainment lawyers in Los Angeles who are knowledgeable in dealing with child actors under the strict California child labor laws. Vic came up with two marvelous young attorneys, Harry Sloan and Larry Kuppin. Gary, Willie and I loved them right away, and they became very, very important in our lives.

In the meantime, a ferment indeed was going on. At Tandem, the new leadership team, Burton and Horn, had exhausted every possibility of finding a new series for Conrad Bain, which they were required to do contractually after the demise of *Maude* in the spring of 1978. Bain had the right to refuse any idea he found terrible, and he had found all of them terrible. In one concept, the extremely intellectual Bain was to be the proprietor of a hangout where kids in the rock music business congregated. In another, he was to be the proprietor of a drugstore. "No, no, no," Bain had said to all of these ideas.

Bain delights in telling the story of what happened after that. He says, "Finally, Al Burton came to me and said, 'You know, we've got another person under contract. Do you know Gary Coleman?' I said I didn't, and they showed me a tape of one of Gary's guest appearances in *The Jeffersons*. I said, 'You didn't warn me that this person is a ten-year-old child who looks six, but he seems like a nice enough little fellow.' They said, 'Good. Let's talk about you two guys doing something together.' I said OK, but the series ideas kept getting worse. Like one in which I was supposed to be a carnival medicine man, with Gary as my shill. I hadn't even met Gary yet, but I personally had to keep saying no, no, no.

"Later they came up with an idea that seemed to be workable. It was called *45 Minutes from Harlem*, and it was about a rich man in the posh community of Hastings-on-Hudson, New York, who adopts a black kid from the Harlem ghetto. ABC bought the concept and writers went to work on it. Unfortunately, the basically charming idea got all fouled up. There was no character development —just gimmicks, *shtik* and pratfalls. They even had a sexy young housekeeper to provide tits-and-ass and jiggle. 'No, no, no,' I said once more. ABC dropped the entire deal. It didn't help that Fred Silverman, who had been after Gary for two years, now had gone on to NBC. His successors at ABC didn't want to cultivate *anything* that had germinated in Silverman's mind."

It was then that Bain himself got into the development act. Tandem's Al Burton gloomily remarked to him, "The best thing to do now, I guess, is to go to Silverman at NBC, but we don't have anything left but you, Gary and an idea. Do you know of anybody who can salvage this mess?" Bain said, "I do indeed," and he recommended Budd Grossman, one of the good writers from the early days of the *Maude* series. Also, Grossman previously had done *Dennis the Menace* and knew how to write for a precocious child. Coincidentally, he was not averse to accepting suggestions from Bain.

Bain's recommendation and suggestions paid off. A delighted Silverman okayed Grossman to write the pilot script for an evolution of *45 Minutes from Harlem* into a similar concept called *Diff'rent Strokes*. In the evolution, Gary acquired a brother (Todd Bridges) and the rich-man character (Bain) now was living on Park Avenue with his teenage daughter and a middle-aged housekeeper—all with well-defined, believable personalities.

But the behind-the-scenes drama wasn't over yet. Bain reports: "Long before Budd Grossman had finished the script, NBC called and asked if Tandem could send over just a few pages so that I could do a scene or two for them with Gary and Todd. We all met at eleven-thirty the next morning in a conference room at NBC in Burbank. It was the first time I really had met either of the two children. We nervously read a few fragments of the uncompleted script for Fred Silverman's right-hand man, Brandon Tartikoff, and other NBC executives."

The reading took about twenty minutes, after which Bain rushed to the hospital to see his daughter, Jennyfer, then twenty-two, who was suffering a severe case of pneumonia. At 1:30 P.M. the phone rang in Jennyfer's room. She pulled off her breathing apparatus, answered the phone and said to her father, "It's for you." Still berating Jennyfer for removing her oxygen mask, Bain picked up the phone and recognized the unmistakable voice of Norman Lear. "Congratulations," said Lear. "NBC just bought *Diff'rent Strokes*. We don't even have to make a pilot. We start on the air November 3, which is three months from now."

Stunned, Bain looked at his watch. It was just one hour and forty minutes since the impromptu reading in the NBC conference room.

Today, Fred Silverman uses this incident as a prime weapon against other producers who come in with requests from NBC for hundreds of thousands of dollars to make a series pilot. Says Silverman, "When they come in asking for money like that, I sit them down and I say, 'Do you know what was my first and only hit show in my first season at NBC?' They say *'Diff'rent Strokes'* and I say 'Right.' Then I say, 'Do you know how *Diff'rent Strokes* got on the air?' They say, 'How?' I say, 'With a twenty minute reading in an office.' They invariably ask, 'No pilot?' I invariably reply, 'No pilot, so this first hit show of mine cost nothing, zilch, in production costs. Now tell me again how much money you say you need to make a pilot to sell me your show.' "

19

Sue got the news about *Diff'rent Strokes* being bought by NBC in an even more bizarre way than had Conrad Bain. She had gone to the network building in Burbank with Gary, but she was asked to wait in the ground-floor reception area while the reading went on upstairs. She was engaged in a conversation with another woman about the high cost of housing in Los Angeles when the elevator door opened and out flew Al Burton. He rushed up to Sue, pumped her hand up and down, kissed her on the cheek and said, "We've got a show, we've got a show!" He explained how the series would begin on November 3, without a pilot, and then hastened back into the elevator.

Sue

I didn't know whether to laugh or cry. It had been such a nerve-wracking time for us. It seems like they were calling us out to Hollywood from Zion every other week that summer, so Gary could read with one kid or another to play his older brother in the script. It was just a few days earlier that the Tandem people had chosen Todd Bridges, who already had some experience playing in the *Fish* series with Abe Vigoda. Vic Perillo had warned me that even with the cast set—they had picked Dana Plato to play Conrad Bain's daughter and Charlotte Rae to play the housekeeper—the pilot would have to be made and then there would be another long period of waiting while the network made up its mind.

But now, the network made up its mind *already*. I could hardly believe it. Gary came down and we kissed each other, and I cried. Then we rushed back to our motel and I called Willie and I cried some more. Willie is the take-charge guy and he said he'd immediately get on the phone to Vic Perillo and our new lawyers, Harry Sloan and Larry Kuppin, to work out the financial arrangements. With all that skill on our side, the deal was soon set with Tandem and NBC. Gary would be getting sixteen hundred dollars an episode. That was more money than any of the Colemans or Lovelaces had ever dreamed of making. Under California's Coogan Law to protect child actors, twenty-five percent of Gary's salary would have to be put into trust for him until he's an adult.

I didn't think too much about the finances. We had to get back to Zion because there were so many things to do. I had to make arrangements with Gary's school to coordinate with Louis Smallwood, who was going to be the tutor for all the children in *Diff'rent Strokes*. I had to work things out with Children's Memorial in Chicago so that Gary would not miss a single checkup, either there or at Children's Hospital in Los Angeles. We had to speed things up with Gary's dentist, Dr. Lawrence Cooper in Waukegan, because a new problem had developed. Just as not enough calcium was going into the bones to make Gary grow, his teeth, too, were not getting enough calcium. They were crumbly and they all had to be strengthened with a synthetic porcelain substance.

Since there was no question that Willie would not give up his job at Abbott, we had to arrange for him to come out to be with us in L.A. as often as possible on weekends. I had to go to Victory Memorial to resign my job after eleven years of nursing there. That called for a lot of tears, too. Many of the nurses were baseball fans and at least I got a laugh out of them by telling them my new job was to be Designated Mother on the Gary Coleman team. I didn't have to remind them that I would continue to be Designated Nurse, as well.

Having done all this, Gary and I returned to Los Angeles in October. I rented a little apartment near the studio and the actor and Designated Mother were ready to go to work.

Production began on *Diff'rent Strokes* the first week in October. Simultaneously, Fred Silverman undertook one of the cleverest promotion campaigns in the history of television. Since no one knew who Gary Coleman was, NBC had the child tape a series of spots which appeared on screen, between innings of the World Series, as "the wit and wisdom of Mr. Gary Coleman." Expecting some adult pundit, the huge NBC baseball audience for the Yankees-Dodgers then were exposed to a close-up of this little boy, spouting such one-liners as "The world would be better if everyone had a hot lunch and a teddy bear."

Next, there was a now-famous appearance for Gary on NBC's *Tonight Show* with Johnny Carson. Sitting on a chair with his tiny legs unable to reach the floor, Gary broke up the audience by discussing the nuclear power controversy. Every time he used erudite words like "offensive" or "designate," he precipitated the patented Johnny Carson deadpan look of disbelief, and the studio audience roared. But the best was yet to come.

Gary

Mr. Carson asked me to tell him about my new

situation comedy but he couldn't remember the title. While he was fumbling around, I said, "You forgot the name already?" He looked embarrassed, like he can do, and everyone laughed. Then he asked me to tell him the plot of *Diff'rent Strokes* which he knew the name now because he found it on a card.

I told him that in the show I was Arnold Jackson from Harlem and I had an older brother, Willis, and when our mother died, we went to live with this rich white man on Park Avenue, where our mother had been his housekeeper. I said, "There's a period of adjustment to Park Avenue for Willis and me, but then we begin to interrelate to this place."

I always talk like that, but when the audience heard me say those words, they really went crazy. I gave them a big grin and Mr. Carson said, "Would you like to take over the show?" I just kept grinning and I gave it a brief pause and I said, "With all the laughing and cheering out there—quite possibly."

The final phase of the Silverman strategy was to have Gary meet the press in selected cities before the initial air date of the show. In Atlanta, there was an unpleasant experience. A reporter got up and asked, "Are you a midget?" The other journalists gasped but Gary coolly looked all around him in a slow take and said, "Are you addressing someone else in the room that I don't see here?" That endeared him to all the reporters, save one. Reams of glowing copy were written about what *Newsweek* called "NBC's Littlest Big Man."

With all this advance hype, *Diff'rent Strokes* got

off to a satisfactory start in NBC's otherwise weak schedule. It continued that way throughout the rest of the season. While it was not quite in the Top Ten in the Nielsen ratings, it hovered in a very respectable range a few notches below. The series was a financial success and Gary Coleman was a star. Later, as the show grew stronger, it performed what was generally considered to be an impossible feat. It was positioned in the schedule opposite the very hot *Charlie's Angels*. To the amazement of the industry, Conrad Bain and the kids clobbered the jiggle ladies.

Sue

From the very beginning, *Diff'rent Strokes* was a very happy set. Gary got along beautifully with the other children. Todd Bridges, who is black, and Dana Plato, who is white, became like an older brother and sister to him. They worked together, they played together and they went to school with Mr. Smallwood together. By law, the children in the entertainment industry can work only four hours a day. In between, there has to be one hour of recreation and three hours of school. Louis Smallwood holds class in a conference room downstairs from the sound stage. Each child works at his own pace. With Gary, Louis uses the same books and materials that his own classmates are using in his home school.

Between Connie Bain and Gary, there was immediate love. Connie's wife told him, "You seem to have acquired an instant grandchild." Gary, who is that strange mixture of semi-adult and child, would be discussing some technical point of acting with Connie. Then in the next minute, he'd be climbing all over him, pulling his nose, poking into his mouth to look at his teeth, even, one time, rubbing Connie's skin "to see if it's brown underneath." I guess that's because Gary knew Connie is so interested in black and minority causes.

It was the same with members of the crew. I'd watch Gary as he talked to them very intelligently about a camera lens or a prop. A few seconds later, the same crew member would have to grab Gary and carry him back, squirming, onto the set, because he was tightrope walking on an electrical cable or trying to raid the padlocked refrigerator backstage.

Gary

When I first started working on *Diff'rent Strokes*, it was hard work, and only once in a while, was it fun. I had never worked on the same thing, day in and day out for month after month, and it took me a while to get used to the routine. Also, we had changes in directors and writers and sometimes things really got messed up. It wasn't only me. The other kids, Todd Bridges and Dana Plato, had a tough time, too.

Dana and Todd are three or four years older than me, and they kinda hung out together. But in only a couple of weeks or so, they got used to having a pesky little kid like me around—remember I was only ten then—and they kinda got to be like my older brother and sister. Todd especially. He's a genius at building things. While we fooled around between shots, he'd find little pieces of things on the set and he'd make robots, space ships, planes, anything you could think of. He was the engineer and electrician, and he'd let me be his helper. We even rigged up an electric alarm system so the assistant director could just press a button and call us back on the set from the classroom, when they needed us to go back to work. Todd got to be my best friend when I just arrived from Zion and didn't know anyone else in L.A.

But from the very beginning, Conrad Bain was the one I really loved. People ask me if I think of Connie like he's a grandpa or an uncle, but none of those things are right. He's more a best friend, like your cat or your dog. Only he can talk. And he's forgot more about acting than most other actors know. Man, he's a good actor. He's like the colonel of our group and the rest of us are lieutenants and privates. I'll say a line, and he'll cock his head kinda sideways and he'll say, "That doesn't sound right to my ear. Try it with this extra word, or put the emphasis on the end of the sentence instead of the beginning." He's always right. The director does that, too, but Connie seems to swing a lot of weight in the production and he always has the last word.

Me and Connie go out to lunch a lot when we're working. I just like a hamburger at Jack-in-the-Box and sometimes we go there; but he likes to sit down at a table in a fancy restaurant, and if that's what the colonel wants, that's where we'll go. Connie teases me a lot because even in the fanciest restaurant, I'll order the same old thing —a hamburger with fries and ketchup. He says, "Young man, your culinary tastes are deplorable," or something high-falutin like that.

Connie is that way with all the kids. For example, he and his wife will invite us up to their house for lunch on a Saturday and then take us to the theater to see a play like *Evolution of the Blues*. Then he'll talk to us about the play all the next week while we're working on the show. What I can say about Connie most of all is that he's a best friend I admire a whole lot.

Sue

When it came to the show, I tried to keep out of the way and not be a stage mother—and I tried not to forget that Gary is, after all, just a child. That's tough to do when you see him accomplish incredible mental things like memorizing an entire fifty-page script in an evening. But I'd spank him when he was naughty, even on the set, which embarrassed him terribly. If it got too bad, I'd ask for Willie to come out for a weekend and impose a little good-old-fashioned fatherly discipline.

On the other hand, I made sure that Gary got to do all the things other little boys do. When he got up at six o'clock every morning, he could watch Woody Woodpecker cartoons on TV while I fixed him breakfast. On his days off, we went to museums and toy stores and movies and amusement parks. Once in a while, we'd spend the day with Harry Sloan—he's one of our lawyers—who has a house sort of in the country. There, Gary would have a ball doing things he'd never done in Zion, like chasing southern California lizards, or slam-dunking a basketball from on top of Vic Perillo's shoulders.

Most of all, he still wanted to collect model trains and to watch the real thing go by on the Southern Pacific tracks all around L.A. We spent a lot of time doing both. By now, too, he was very interested in electronic games. I bought him games where you shoot down space ships, games where you play blackjack, games where you play hockey. He made me compete with him in all of them. He always won.

But the biggest interest for him continued to be the trains. And that's why his present for his twelfth birthday turned out to be one of the most unusual gifts a little boy ever received.

Gary already had all the toys he could play with after his kidney's birthday on December 18 and

A GIFT OF LIFE

Christmas on December 25. Just before his birthday on February 8, we went home to Zion to be with Willie because we had been running up such astronomical phone bills talking on the phone. Willie came back to Los Angeles with us.

It was a dreary February Saturday and the rain was coming down in buckets. We were packing clothes, and Gary wanted to know where we were going. Willie said, "We've got to go out to NBC in Burbank and you might have to sit for some publicity pictures there." Gary got upset immediately, saying, "I don't want to do pictures," whining a little.

We got picked up by big Vic Stringer, Gary's friend and protector. Vic drove us to the area around Union Station in downtown L.A. Then Vic pretended to get lost and ended up among the box cars. Vic said, "I'd better ask someone how to get to NBC from here." He went into the Post Office and came out. He said, "I don't think that guy knew what he was talking about. Maybe I'd better go in the train station and get directions." So he went into the train station and Gary was antsy. Vic came out and said, "Yes, we're going the right way now, but we have a few minutes, so let's go in the station and have a cup of coffee."

Gary said he didn't want any coffee, but we went into the station anyway. Gary ran off saying, "As long as I'm here, I'm going to see the trains." Willie and I yelled to him to come back and we handed him an envelope. It was from Vic Perillo. Gary said, "Oh, it's just a birthday card. I'll look at it when I come back from seeing the trains." I said, "Open it." He did, and there was a set of tickets for all of us to take the AMTRAK train all the way to San Diego and back. Gary let out a whoop of delight that echoed all the way through that train station.

The AMTRAK people were in on it, too, and they let Gary go up in the locomotive and talk to the engineer before we got started. He was never so excited in his life. Then, on the trip itself, Gary was briefed on the grades and crossings and speed limits by the conductor, and his little face was glued to the window for nearly every minute, going and coming, except for when he was eating.

When we got back to Union Station in Los Angeles that night, Gary threw his arms around us and thanked us. With all his being a TV star and everything that went with it, he said, "I love you, Mom and Dad. Today was the best thing that ever happened to me."

Gary

Why do I love trains? I like anything that moves —trucks, cars, ships, planes—but my favorite is trains. They're styled just right for this era. What could be more beautiful than a big SD-40 diesel sliding along out of Chicago across the prairies and the mountains and deserts, on its way to L.A.? Or even the E60CP Electric going at a hundred miles an hour on the Metroliner between

A GIFT OF LIFE

New York and Washington, with its two pantographs, one in the back and one in the front, pulling in electricity from the overhead wires. I love how trains sound. They have horns and make noise. I love anything that makes noise.

But I also love anything that helps the United States, and that's what trains do. With oil running out, the cheapest way to use oil is in the big diesels. And trains are the nice easy way to go. You look out the window and you see the most wonderful things in every mile. Maybe if more people took trains and really *saw* America, they wouldn't treat it so badly when it comes to the environment and all.

I have more model trains than a lot of kids, but to tell you the truth, I've only been on *real* trains twice. The first time was when I was doing commercials in Chicago and rode the Chicago and Northwestern. The second time was when I made that wonderful trip from L.A. to San Diego and back with Mom and Dad. I got so disappointed when I heard on the news that AMTRAK might only have another two years to go, because I still have so much to experience on trains. I've never been in a sleeping car; I've never ridden a Superliner, which is the best railroad passenger car there is; I've never eaten in a real dining car, like the models I have at home. Grandpa has a friend who drives an engine taking a string of freight cars from Lima to Cincinnati three times a week, and he promised me I could ride in the engineer's cab on that run, sometime. I can't wait.

If trains are still around when I grow up, and if for any reason I don't stay in show business, what I think I'd like best is to be a train engineer.

But on the other hand, I'm an electronics freak, and next to trains, I like electronic toys and calculators best. Also, I was born in 1968, so I was able to see the last moon launching on television, and that was the most exciting thing in my life.

So maybe I might end up being a space scientist.

20

By now, the Colemans had gone through a considerable change in their lives. For one thing, they had become rich. In the spring of 1979, when it was obvious that *Diff'rent Strokes* was a hit and that Gary was extremely instrumental to its success, the show was eagerly renewed for the 1979-80 season by NBC. At that point the Colemans' skilled negotiating team of Perillo-Sloan-Kuppin had moved into action. They were not unlike the agents and lawyers for a rookie quarterback in the National Football League who saves a franchise with his brilliant play in his first year, but is only earning one-tenth the salary of other NFL quarterbacks.

Gary's negotiators pointed out that Gary's $1,600 per episode seemed pitiful compared with the $25,000 to $50,000 earned by most other hit-series stars. As is the custom in such entertainment industry labor squabbles, there was a lot of sound and fury, screaming and yelling, threats of lawsuits and countersuits, even the possibility that Gary would not show up for the start of production in July. As is also the custom in such squabbles, there was a last-minute settlement. Gary's new salary was never announced, but in California, all children's contracts must be approved by a judge of the Superior Court. The overall amount then becomes a part of the public record. By agreement with Tandem, the exact figure cannot be published, but Gary now makes a considerable sum, in the same league, say, with a good NFL quarterback. Twenty-five percent of that, of course, goes into trust for Gary's future.

But then Perillo, Sloan and Kuppin got together and decided they must move further to assure that Gary would never fade into poverty again, as has happened with so many other child actors. Perillo says, "Concerning what we did, let me say this: I do not take the credit for discovering Gary, only for guiding him. Ninety-nine percent of what makes this child such a unique and successful human being comes from his parents. He got the fearlessness from his father, the compassion and understanding from his mother, his instinctive acting talent—without a single lesson—from somewhere in his genes. The child is so sensitive that the last thing we wanted was for him to get bored or fed up with acting one day and say, 'I don't want to do this anymore' leaving him with nothing else to fall back on.

"So we set up a production company for him, Gary Coleman Productions. Gary himself soon changed the name to Zephyr Productions, because two of his favorite old trains were the Burlington

A GIFT OF LIFE

Zephyr and the Denver Zephyr. The first deal we made for this production company was with NBC for one TV-movie a year. The movies could star Gary or not. The first two, *The Kid from Left Field* and *Scout's Honor* were vehicles for Gary; the third, *Evita!—First Lady*, was not. The press had a lot of fun saying that a twelve-year-old kid was producing a film about Eva Perón. They didn't understand that it simply was Gary's *company* making the pictures, with competent professionals doing all the work. By Gary's company, I mean that while we're running it now, with Willie Coleman as president, it becomes Gary's company exclusively, with all its profits, as soon as he gets to be legally an adult at eighteen. Since Gary is already so fascinated with all the behind-the-camera facets of the movie business, we expect that he'll move right in and become a producer, probably also a director, with his own independent company already in existence. That could make him the youngest big-time black producer in the business. If he's not interested in such a career and maybe wants to go into science, his other love, he'll still have a considerable income for life."

The second phase in the evolution of Zephyr Productions, née Gary Coleman Productions, came when Perillo-Sloan-Kuppin made a further deal with 20th Century-Fox to distribute all the company's films produced for the movie theaters rather than for TV. The first of these theatrical releases, starring Gary, was *On the Right Track*.

One of the unexpected beneficiaries of all these developments was the National Kidney Foundation. With Gary now a star and his future unshakably secure, Willie and Sue decided to do whatever they could to help other people—especially children—afflicted with the same disease that Gary had.

Sue

We never had talked much about Gary's medical problems and the kidney transplant, but now we were so grateful to God that we felt it was only our duty to come right out with it. We wanted to let other people see Gary as an example of how a kidney transplant can work. We wanted to encourage other parents who get so frightened when they learn their child needs a transplant or dialysis.

So we began to mention Gary's transplant more and more in the press, and soon we were in contact with the National Kidney Foundation in New York. Gary immediately became their living symbol of how a child can undergo what he went through and still become successful in life. Their big problem is not only to get money to carry on their research and educational programs, but, even more important, to encourage people to become kidney donors. Adults can pledge their kidneys to science, in advance. Parents can be made to understand that if something, God forbid, happens to their child, the child's kidneys can provide "the gift of life" to perhaps two other children. There are maybe fourteen thousand people in the United States who could lead active, healthy lives, like Gary, if enough donor kidneys were available.

In 1979, Gary became the Honorary Gift of Life Chairman of the National Kidney Foundation. He made public appearances for the Foundation; he made little ad lib speeches at their affairs, sometimes conning *me* into making a speech, too, by calling on me to stand up in the audience as "his mom, who made it all possible." The little devil knew the people would clap and insist that I say a few words about how a donor kidney saved my son's life and how important it is for people to become donors. Gary used to tease me about my speeches afterwards, but I'm sure he was proud of me as I overcame my natural shyness and got better and better at it.

Most important of all, Gary did a whole series of public-service television commercials for the Foundation. The spots usually showed Gary running around frenetically, as he usually does, while talking about some kid he knew whose life was saved by a donated kidney. Then he looked right into the camera and said, "*I* am that kid," or "You're *looking* at that kid." The spots have been very successful. The Kidney Foundation people have told me it's many more times easier for them to find donors since Gary has been doing the commercials. One of the Foundation people said, "It's basically a grim subject, but with Gary up there on the screen, it somehow becomes less grim. And people *listen* to him, realizing he's been through it himself and that but for the grace of his transplant, he might not even be around to entertain them."

This kind of volunteer work also opened up a whole new world for Gary. That's how he met Amy Carter, for instance. Ethel Kennedy knew what Gary was doing for the Kidney Foundation, so when she had an affair for the benefit of disturbed children at her home outside Washington, D.C., she invited Gary, as an example of a child who had overcome another kind of handicap. Amy Carter, the then-President's little girl, was there. When she and Gary met, it was one of the cutest things I've ever seen.

Gary

Actually, the only reason I wanted to go to the party was so I could meet Amy, but when we got there she hadn't come in yet. People kept asking me for autographs and I kept signing them, but my eye was on the door so I could see when she came in.

Finally I saw a guy I knew was a Secret Service man because of a button I saw on his coat. I asked him if he was there because Amy was there. He told me he was there because Amy was going to be there but she hadn't arrived yet. He sent me over to another Secret Service man who was sitting next to a fancy kind of radio. He said he was called "base" and that with this radio he

A GIFT OF LIFE

could talk to all the other Secret Service men outside on the grounds who carried walkie-talkies. He knew who I was and asked me for my autograph. Then he asked me if I wanted to talk through the radio to the other Secret Service men outside.

I said I sure would and I picked up the mike and said, "Is Amy here yet?" A lot of guys out there must have known my voice because three or four of them said, "Not yet, Gary."

I talked to "base" for a while and he explained the radio to me, which is something like a CB. Then I heard the voice of the Secret Service man on the gate. He said, "If you can hear me, Gary, Amy's coming in now." I said, "Roger, over and out," and "base" patted me on the back and laughed.

A couple of minutes later, Amy walked in. I was signing autographs again, but I finished up in a hurry to get over to her. Instead, she came right up to me. She shook hands with me and said, "Hi, Gary, I watch you on *Diff'rent Strokes* all the time and it's my favorite show." She was kinda shy, and so was I, I guess, because I never met a President's daughter before. I said, "I watch you on TV all the time, too, when you're traveling around all those countries with your mom and dad and I see you on the news."

She kinda laughed and she asked me if she could have my autograph. I said, "Sure, if you give me *your* autograph." So she signed an autograph for me and I signed one for her. Then we talked a while, about things like school. She told me how much she enjoyed being in a school with a lot of black kids and I told her how much I enjoyed being in a school with a lot of white kids. Later, we toured the White House, and when we passed the kitchen, the cooks were watching *Diff'rent Strokes* on their TV set. So we all went in and watched, too.

I sure do like that Amy. She's real nice—for a girl.

21

Being sensible people, the Colemans found their new affluence did not change their life style as much as you would think. Willie got a new car in Zion, but Sue drove the same Chevrolet Malibu she acquired when she first settled in Los Angeles. While in L.A. for filming and taping, she and Gary now lived in their own rented house instead of in hotels and motels. The house is hardly in the movie star category. It is not in Bel Air. It is not in Beverly Hills. It is in a pleasant, tree-lined, middle-class neighborhood of West Los Angeles, chosen specifically by Sue "because it has sidewalks so Gary can ride his bike, and because it has a lot of children so Gary can have plenty of playmates when he isn't working."

The playmates abound. On his off-days, Gary can be seen scrambling around the neighborhood with perhaps a dozen kids, mostly white and all a foot taller than he is. You can see them roller skating, skate-boarding or playing racquet-ball, one of Gary's favorite activities. It would be fan-magazineish to imply that the other children are not aware that Gary is a big TV and movie star. They watch his shows and ask for his photos. Yet he lives in a little stucco house, just like they do, and he never talks about his work. In truth, he seems to be more admired for his incredible collection of model electric trains, which, at any given time, could be operated by five or six neighborhood kids in the Coleman basement. There is only one stipulation. Gary is the chief engineer, and he wears a genuine railroad engineer's cap to prove it.

With the extra money, there were new clothes for Sue, more visits to the hairdresser, an occasional night out in a restaurant with Gary. But there were no cooks or chauffeurs. She continued to do all the cooking at home to make sure Gary did not stray from his prescribed diet, and she continued to drive Gary to the studio every day.

Sue

With all his vitality, with all his squirming and running and jumping around, it's easy to forget that Gary is a chronically ill child. Any child with a kidney transplant is chronically ill, even though it never shows on the surface. Too many parents

A GIFT OF LIFE

of children with transplants get lulled into a false sense of security. They forget the daily medications that prevent rejection; they let the child have too much salt on his food—and there's trouble.

I would never allow myself to fall into that trap. It's a duty and it must be faced. Sometimes I wake up in the morning with that flat feeling that "Lord, it's still here and it won't go away." But I pull myself together and prepare Gary's medications and cook his breakfast properly. It's what I have to do and I do it.

It doesn't happen so much anymore, but I used to wake up with the dread that something might be wrong with him. With a kidney child, you even worry about a little thing like his catching a cold. There's always the warning signs that the body's defense mechanisms might be out of balance. So the least thing, even a cold, brings it to mind again.

That's why I'm with him all the time. That's why *I* give him his medication. Once someone said to me, "Why don't you let him travel by himself? People are very good; they take care of him on the airlines." But I said, "I'll never be away from him, not so long as he has to take those medications." When he's old enough, when I'm sure he knows what he's doing, only then will I let him do it himself. But when he's fifty years old, I'll probably still be calling him up and saying, "Did you take your pills today?"

Am I being overprotective? The doctors don't think so and they actually commend me for it. But Gary thinks otherwise. Sometimes he gets so mad at me that he locks himself in his room and won't talk to me. On the other hand, I'm moody, too, and I won't talk to him for hours at a time. But my moods I can handle. His I never know about, and that's part of the problem I face every day. The medications he takes sometimes cause depression and aggressiveness, and I have to get on the phone right away to ask the doctors if there should be a change in the dosages.

But with all his mood swings, Gary basically is a very loving child, both to Willie and me. With all the money he makes, he's a minor and can't get his hands on it. So he'll think up all kinds of ingenious ways to buy little things that will express his love for us.

For example, just before Mother's Day in 1980, I sensed that Gary was involved in all sorts of mysterious activity. But I didn't find out until later what he was up to.

Gary

It all started when I was talking with Mom one day and I was asking her why girls played with dolls. She explained that girls played with dolls for the same reason that I played with trains. They were make-believe mommies with their babies, just like I was a make-believe engineer at the throttle of a big AMTRAK diesel hauling a string of freight cars. Since Mom is a girl, I asked her how long it was since she had a doll. She said, "Oh, about twenty-five years."

That gave me an idea. I had a toy catalogue from F.A.O. Schwartz in New York, because when Dad bought me something there once, I wrote my name down on a list so they would keep sending me their catalogue in the mail.

So I took out the latest one and I began looking through it. There were all kinds of dumb dolls that go "coo-coo" and "goo-goo" like little babies, and there were dolls you could dress up in all kinds of clothes. But I didn't see anything that was good enough for Mom. Then, way in the back of the catalogue, on a full page by itself, there was a doll that really flipped me out.

The catalogue said this doll was made out of China porcelain. It was so beautiful, it reminded me of things I saw once on a school field trip to the Marshall Field Museum. The only problem was the price. It cost ninety dollars, with sales tax and handling. Even if I used my whole allowance, without buying things like soda pop and bubble gum, it would take me three years to save up for it.

So I had to figure out some other way. I cut the page out of the catalogue and I put it in an envelope with a letter to Anita de Thomas, who is the business manager for our production company. In the letter, I told Anita I wanted to buy this doll for Mom, and because I didn't have any money, was there any way she could handle it. I then sealed up the envelope.

But I had another problem. How was I going to get this to Anita? I wasn't sure I had the right address and I didn't want to tip anybody off by asking for it, so I couldn't send it in the mail. So I just wrote Anita's name on the envelope and I asked Mom if she could deliver it for me. I told Mom she was not to open the envelope under any circumstances, under penalty of death.

Mom kind of smiled and she later promised me that she delivered the envelope to Anita without opening it.

About a week later, this package arrived by United Parcel Service from F.A.O. Schwartz. I was so excited that I couldn't help myself and I showed it to Mom. Then I hid it. For days, Mom kept asking me what was in the package and I kept saying, "You want to know what it is so badly, but I'm not going to tell you." Then I got her off the track by saying it was a present for me from Vic Perillo. Then I kept teasing her by saying, "I'm *still* not going to tell you what it is."

I could hardly wait for Mother's Day. It came, and it was Sunday, so Mom slept late. I made a big production of waking her up with music from my record player. Then I gave her the package. She opened it, and there was the doll, just like in the catalogue, all dressed up in old-fashioned clothes. Mom picked me up and hugged me and said it was the most beautiful doll she had ever seen in her whole life.

I guess she really does like it, because she keeps it on her dresser all the time, either in Los Angeles or in Zion.

• • •

A GIFT OF LIFE 183

In Zion, the new Coleman affluence had changed things considerably, unlike the Los Angeles situation. It also precipitated a crisis involving Willie.

First, they bought a new house. With Gary's celebrity, they really had outgrown the little yellow bungalow on 31st Street. It was literally overrun with children who came to see Gary and play with him when he was home, which was several months a year, what with the vacation times and hiatus periods of television production; also Sue's desire to get Gary back to his home school in Zion as often as possible.

One day, Willie heard about a house for sale in one of the most desirable residential areas of Zion. Sue and Gary then were in Los Angeles. Willie went over to look at the house and discovered that it was owned by the same real estate broker, James Paxton, who had gotten them their first house. Paxton was now retired and out of the city, but his son, John, told Willie, "Mr. Coleman, it would be a pleasure for me to sell my dad's house to you. Once again, we have a situation where it's an all-white area, but I can assure you the neighbors will welcome you."

Willie was overwhelmed with the home. It was a modern brick-wood-and-glass structure with six bedrooms, four fireplaces and a downstairs area that could be Gary's exclusive province. There was a beautiful garden in front and an acre of lawn and trees in the back, with a lovely brook bordering the property. The price was gratifyingly low for these days of soaring real estate values. And the mortgage interest rates had not yet begun to zoom.

Willie phoned Sue and his enthusiasm was such that it instantaneously became contagious. The pragmatic Sue suggested sending one of their business advisers to look at it. The adviser, Sue Rittenhouse, was dispatched. Sue's evaluation: "At that price, it's such an incredible investment that you'd be crazy if you didn't buy it." Willie began the procedures to purchase the house. Sue and Gary could scarcely wait until the Thanksgiving break in TV production to get back to Zion to see it. It exceeded their wildest expectations.

They moved in soon thereafter. They acquired, as their next-door neighbor, the mayor's brother, whose thirteen-year-old son became an instant buddy of Gary's. Before long, the Coleman house once again was swarming with the children of this new neighborhood, but now they could be confined to Gary's downstairs living quarters, playroom and Model Train Emporium.

Sue

The new house, in a way, was tied in with the crisis that Willie faced. When Gary's production company was formed, Willie sat in on many of the discussions and he became quite knowledgeable about show business. He had to. As president of the company, sitting in for Gary until he gets old enough to take over, it was necessary for Willie to understand and approve everything that Vic Perillo, Harry Sloan and Larry Kuppin were doing. With Willie's stubbornness and quick mind, he and the others made a good team.

When Gary made his first TV movie, *The Kid from Left Field*, Willie got a leave of absence from Abbott and came out to Los Angeles to be present on the set and at the locations. But he isn't like me. I can sit around all day just keeping an eye on Gary when he's working. Willie found that once a director has taken over production, there's little for someone like him to do. He was miserable. And he didn't like the weather, or the social pressures, or the spread-out geography of southern California.

People kept saying to him, "You certainly don't need the money now. Why don't you give up your job at Abbott and stay in California full-time working with Gary like Sue does?"

That was his crisis—and mine, too, in a way. On the one hand, nothing would make me happier than having Willie with us full-time. We could be an all-year-round family unit again. On the other hand, I thought of all the parents in show business who become satellites of their children, who simply live off them. Even though Willie would be involved in the business decisions, there wouldn't be enough to do and he'd end up mostly as Gary's driver and bodyguard. That would be demeaning for him.

With all the distance he's come from being a share cropper in Mississippi, my husband is a proud man. He has to be his *own* man. At the Abbott Laboratories, he's liked and respected. He does a very important job. He's advanced a long way.

Willie kept asking me what he should do, and I kept stalling. That led to one of our classic fights, where I keep thinking over both sides of a question and he keeps demanding an answer. I knew the answer, but I was being selfish because I wanted him with us in Los Angeles.

Finally I said to him, "All right, *you* give me the answer, and if I think it's the right decision, I'll back you up."

He said, "I don't want to give up my job at Abbott. All the money in the world doesn't mean anything unless a man feels useful doing the work he knows how to do best. I would like us to keep living in the house in Zion. I would like that to be our permanent home, with you and Gary being there as often as possible. I could always come where I'm needed to make the business decisions for Gary."

I said, "You've made the right decision."

Willie said, "Like we always do, let's ask Gary."

We called Gary in and he snapped right out with his answer—short and to the point. Gary said, "Daddy should keep his job at Abbott's and we should keep our house in Zion."

Willie

I've never been prouder of my son than at that moment. I always said that God seems to be repaying Gary for what he's gone through with his kidney. The Lord took something away and He gave something back—Gary's intelligence, his ability to cope with life, and, most of all, his talent to entertain people and make them laugh.

And now I also knew that in making Gary so smart, He also gave him understanding.

22

How smart *is* Gary?

Based on that early IQ test at Children's Memorial in Chicago when he was only five years old, he probably would be rated a genius. Later IQ's at Shiloh Park School in Zion place him below that level. Principal Robert Fink says, "Gary scored in the 135 to 137 range. The highest we ever had with any child on these particular tests was a 140. Whether or not you put any stock in this sort of thing, Gary is a very, very bright boy. "His test score puts him in the top two and a half percent of the population.

The word "genius" keeps popping up in Gary's many guest appearances with such talk-show hosts as Johnny Carson and Merv Griffin. This is understandable. He knows many polysyllabic and technical words which he uses freely and with total understanding. He also speaks in complete, grammatical sentences which actually can be parsed, unlike those of most presidential candidates. Such ad-libbed repartee endears Gary to both the talk-show host and the audiences. Dr. Ira Greifer says, "It's all the more startling to hear all this brightness coming from the mouth of such a little guy." In retrospect, he's right. Another precocious child-actor, Brooke Shields, did very well on the talk-shows when she was thirteen years old, but, as Dr. Greifer puts it, "somehow a smart five-foot-ten inch child doesn't seem as smart as a smart three-foot-ten-inch child."

Nonetheless, Gary continues to enchant not only the Carsons and the Griffins, but also other intelligent actors with whom he has worked, such as Steve Allen. In 1979, he co-hosted NBC's *The Big Show* with Allen and he did a guest spot in a Lucille Ball special, in which he played a miniature Fred Silverman in a skit. Both Allen and Miss Ball adore him to this day. But sometimes Gary doesn't do so well. Says his agent, Vic Perillo, "The child is so bright that he has great sensitivity and when someone doesn't relate to him on the air, or talks down to him, he responds in kind. That's what happened when he was on with Bill Cosby and also with George Carlin. Cosby seemed to be competing with him and treating him as just another little kid, like those in Bill's pudding commercials. Carlin provoked Gary into a discussion about the Hollywood sound-stage tutors being better than the public schools in Zion." Principal Robert Fink says, "Gary was so upset about that exchange having taken place that he phoned all the way from Los Angeles the next day to apologize."

In school, Gary is a straight-A student—except in math. Fink says, "Right now, simple arithmetic bores him, but when he gets into algebra and geometry, I'm sure his interest and his grades will pick up, because math then becomes puzzle-solving, which fascinates him."

Even so, says Fink, "Gary in the sixth grade actually was working at eighth grade level." In 1980, Illinois state law required Gary to shift his educational base to California, since he was not putting in a sufficient number of actual classroom hours in Zion. He then was enrolled in the International Children's School in Los Angeles for the periods when he was in California, even though he would still be taught by Louis Smallwood and other tutors on TV and movie sets. International Children's, a private school, immediately and independently confirmed Fink's evaluation. From the sixth grade, Gary moved into a combined seventh-and-eighth grade curriculum.

But the most significant indication of Gary's intelligence, perhaps, is in his writing. Some of his compositions are typed, since he learned to use a typewriter at the age of eight; others are in his own distinctive, bold handwriting.

The following poem was typed:

Differences Between Suburb and City

> I live in the city,
> Noisy, nasty and crazy.
> Trucks parked in the street,
> And troubled cops on the beat.
>
> Live in the city,
> Poor people live in such pity.
> They get harassed;
> And thieves steal their hash.

> But I live in the country.
> Away from torment,
> And scornment.
>
> But I live in the country.
> Away from thieves,
> That make poor people grieve.
>
> So compare the city,
> Compare the suburb,
> Pick the likeable,
> Pick the city,
> Full of pity.
> Pick the country,
> Be a sentry in the Army,
> Because you never lived in the city . . .
> To turn crazy. . . .
>
> —Gary Coleman

Hardly William Wordsworth or even Allen Ginsberg, but quite remarkable for an eleven-year-old, which is what Gary was when he wrote it.

In 1980, Gary starred in the TV-movie, *Scout's Honor*, as part of the deal with NBC. The director of the film was Henry Levin, a middle-aged former child star. Gary took to Levin immediately. He would sit on the director's lap, listening to tales of the old days in the theater in New York. Also, Levin filled Gary in on all the intricacies of the art of directing film, which always had fascinated the child.

The day after filming was completed, Levin had a massive heart attack and died. Gary was bereft. As close as he had been to it himself, the death of someone near to him was something he did not know how to handle. He grieved for days, saying "But there still was so much for him to teach me." Except for a few words of comfort, Willie and Sue left Gary to work it out by himself.

On the eighth day, Gary gave the following handwritten letter to his father and mother:

*A Letter of Words That
Cannot Be Expressed Vocally*
Henry Levin 5/1/80

Mom-Dad:

You are right about you can't bring back the dead and tears are useless. But this was a man of great honesty and usefulness. He—to me—was a man of power and no one would even know or care if he . . . *Is*, I should say, because, you see, his blood lives within me, his thoughts, his ideas, his beliefs, his worthiness to live, to have a life on earth and to enjoy living. His soul is in my heart and no one is going to convince me different. I loved that man, I wanted to know him better, but God wouldn't allow it. Like you said, He may have needed him for a purpose. But to me, what "purpose" was so important that it couldn't wait for me to spend time with him, and to talk to him, and to understand him more. But now he's gone. You know, it hurts real bad. I've been trying to cover up for it all week by getting excited about Mother's Day and to give the gift to Mom, but now I see that is hard to do because of the anguish and pain I feel mostly in my heart. I can't talk about this aloud to you because I may get terribly upset. But I'm alright enough, I think, to write this little note telling how it really feels to know someone is gone, "been called for." It makes you kind of angry at

God. You're not supposed to be like that. You're supposed to look at it like "making room for someone else's place on earth." You're supposed to cheer for the dead and boo at the born. The dead are going on to heaven and getting off earth. The born are coming to earth where unhappiness, evilness prevails. But anyway, I know I'll get over it soon, later, or in between. But Henry Levin was an absolute beautiful person. He *is*. I'll think of him but never, never, ever forget him. He was—*is*—great. I'm sorry. And this is the end of a mournful week for me.

Your son,
Gary   Thursday, 4:30

There are still other ways of evaluating Gary's intelligence. From his random snippets of conversation, for example.

Consider the following, from a boy who was just barely twelve years old at the time:

Gary

I'm glad we're still living in Zion because it's important for Dad to have his own career. But it's also good for me to be able to live in two places.

L.A. is all right, but in downtown Hollywood, there's a lot of burglars and muggers and people who do dumb things. There are gangs, there's scribbling all over the walls, and nasty movies. It's nice where I live, but the traffic problem is immense in L.A. Transportation is impossible there. There are no El's, no decent buses. Everything is too big and spread out. I like to be scrunched in.

I have two sets of friends. In L.A., my best friend is Charlie, who lives across the street, but most of my friends are in Zion. There's Kyle, Bobby and Jason, the mayor's nephew, who lives next door. We ride our bikes all over the place, and we play in my backyard, and splash around in the creek. Sometimes we walk about a half mile to Lake Michigan and hang out there on the beach. Their parents let them stay over at my house, and I stay over at their's. They come to play with my trains and I go to their houses for darts, archery and racquet ball, at which I am pretty good.

Then we have the girls, who live down the street. There are three of them and everyone calls them The Girls. They're just as good as the guys when it comes to riding bikes or playing racquet ball. The oldest of the girls is Tanya. I really like her because she's a teenager and I can have intelligent conversations with her. I always like girls who are maybe seventeen or eighteen, especially if they're pretty and smart. I hate the *little* girls my own age because they say dumb things and after a little while, I can't find anything to discuss with them. I'm only twelve years old and they're maybe eleven, but they say dumb things to me like, "I'm going to marry you for your money." I tell them my allowance is only two dollars and fifty cents a week, and then I run away to the guys.

A GIFT OF LIFE

Two of my best friends are my dogs. We started with Champion, the German shepherd, when I was only a little baby and we practically grew up together. We used to roughhouse around in the yard, but then he got too big for me and knocked me down a lot. Then Mom wouldn't let me roughhouse with Champion anymore. He's still the best watchdog in the world, though.

In March of 1980, we had big storms and floods in L.A. The wind blew the gate open and Champion got away. Mom and I drove all up and down the streets calling his name and asking people about him, but we couldn't find him anywhere. I was so broke up, I thought I was about to die.

I went to work one day and Dana Plato, who's in the show with me, brought her dog into the studio with her. The dog was a chihuahua, a teentsy little thing named Kita, and she was the cutest little rascal I've ever seen. I fell in love with her and I rassled with her, and I said to Mom, "Maybe we'd better get a chihuahua like this who's little and more my size to play with. It wouldn't be like Champion, but at least I'd have *someone*." Mom cried a little and said she'd talk it over with Dad. A few days later, she came home with a four-month old chihuahua puppy named Venus. Venus was gray and skinny and no bigger than my size thirteen shoe.

Venus kissed everyone a lot, and she peed in the house, and she tore up her dog bed, but I fell in love with her right away. She almost made me forget Champion.

Then, about two weeks later, Mom got a call from a man in Beverly Hills, about three miles away. The man said a German shepherd who was tired and dirty and hungry had wandered into their yard, but wouldn't let anyone touch him. After a while, he accepted food and they were able to get a look at his collar. They saw a number on his rabies tag and the name of a veterinarian in Zion, Illinois. He called the vet in Zion, who looked up the number and told him who the dog belonged to. We couldn't believe it was Champion after all those weeks, but it was. We rushed over and when Champion saw us, he took off in the air with his whole hundred and twenty pounds, and he knocked me down and kissed me all over on the face.

So now we had Champion *and* Venus. Little Venus bugged him and played with him until she wore him out. Champion was jealous at first and growled at her, but soon he came to love her and watch over her like she was his own little baby.

Now, when I come home from the studio at night, Venus and I spend about an hour chasing each other around the house and playing games with balls. The same thing happens when we're in Zion. Champion lies around outside, watching us through the window and sort of smiling. He even lets Venus do the barking and be the watchdog every once in a while. It just goes to show you how people of such different types can learn how to get along.

When it comes to the difference between making movies and television, it's ridiculous in television where you have to shoot sixty-six pages in five days, with three days rehearsing and two days of camera-blocking and filming. With a movie, you have forty-two days to shoot a hundred pages. Movies or television, I always study my lines at night, just before I go to bed. That way, the lines stay in my head. Otherwise, I might get up in the morning and watch *Star-Blazers* on television, which I always do, and if I studied the lines in the morning, I wouldn't be able to remember them at all.

It's not so terrible to be short, except that you have to stand on a chair or a stool sometimes or jump up to get places. If you ask me if I'd rather be short and smart, or tall and dumb, I'd have to say, "I'll take tall and smart." But I realize now that I don't have any control over that, so I take it like it is.

23

What about Gary's prognosis, or long-range medical forecast, for his health as a kidney-transplant medical miracle?

A nonmedical official of the National Kidney Foundation says, "There's no reason why Gary couldn't live until ninety—if he diligently continues to take his daily immunosuppressive medications."

"Actually," says Dr. Ira Greifer, "no one can say that for sure, since the very first transplant was performed only twenty-seven years ago. That lady is alive and well, so the most we can predict with absolute certainty is that a kidney-transplant recipient can live for twenty-seven years. But we doctors do tend to be ultra-conservative."

That lady, referred to by Dr. Greifer, received her kidney from an identical twin. This is the most clinically successful type of transplant. The antigen factors all match. It's almost like receiving an organ from your own body. Such identical-twin transplants are practically 100 percent trouble-free.

The second best kind of transplant is the "related living donor" type. As the name implies, the kidney comes from a mother, father, a brother, or a sister, with the antigen match as close as possible. With a "related living donor" transplant, the survival rate is from 75 percent to 90 percent.

Today, the unfortunately-titled "cadaver donor" is the most common. When Gary had his "cadaver donor" transplant in 1973, the survival rate was only 40 percent. Says Dr. Greifer, "To be conservative, we still use that figure, but in actuality, there have been so many advances in combating rejection that we are getting 50 to 60 percent successes now, and up to 75 percent in some transplantation centers. As a result, twenty-five hundred to three thousand kidney transplants a year are being done in the United States today."

Continues Dr. Greifer: "And when we say 'successful,' we're talking about that rule-of-thumb criterion of the first two years without rejection. Remember that Gary has had his kidney for eight years now, and after that length of time, anything that happens can be managed. He should live a long and continuingly fruitful life."

Dr. Casimir Firlit, Gary's surgeon, is equally optimistic. He says, "The young man has decades ahead of him. Parental care is exceedingly important from the standpoint of compliance, in terms of the child taking his medication. And Sue Coleman is almost religiously fanatic about this.

"Gary does have some degree of mild chronic rejection, but the important thing to know is that very typically it can go on for a very long time with the proper care, before anything further might have to be done. I don't want to put it in terms of ten years, fifteen years—let's just say 'a bunch of years.' It can go on and on, and the patient would be otherwise healthy."

What's the worst that could happen if, for any reason, it doesn't continue to go on and on and on?

"No big thing," Dr. Firlit says. "We'd just take the kidney out and put another one in. The state of the art progressing the way it is, by the time we had to do anything way off in the future, Gary wouldn't miss more than a few days' work, even if we had to put him on dialysis for a while until a new kidney could be found for him. And the new kidney would be even better. We're in a period of discovery of revolutionary techniques which could make rejection of the kidney, acute *or* chronic, a thing of the past."

In speaking about the advancing state of the art, Dr. Firlit is referred to new, compact, super-efficient dialysis machines that can be used in the home. The patient can be fitted with a device in his arm (not missing "more than a few days' work") and then go about his business during the day—even with no kidney at all—and cleanse his blood by hooking himself to the dialysis machine at home at night. Such patients no longer are restricted or debilitated, no matter what the nature of their work.

Then, when it comes time for a new kidney transplant, a process of desensitization could eventually be employed before the operation is attempted. Dr. Firlit describes this desensitization procedure as analogous to curing a person of an allergy. Says Dr. Firlit, "Even if you don't know the cause of the allergy, you inject the patient with very small doses of all sorts of allergy-causing pollens and substances.

Gradually, the body builds up resistance to all the injected substances, so that when the culprit among them enters the system, it is recognized by the new antibodies in the bloodstream. The antibodies do not attack the invader, and the allergic reaction is averted.

"It could be the same thing viewing a transplanted kidney as a similar invader. We will be able to inject the patient in advance with all possible combinations of antigens, some of which are bound to coincide with the antigens in the new kidney. Then, when it is implanted, the kidney will be recognized by its sister antigens as a friend, not a foe. In effect, the body's defenses will say, 'I know you,' and they will not produce antibodies to attack and destroy it. With lesser dosages of immunosuppressive drugs, the kidney could then live happily in the body as long as the patient does not finally die of some other cause."

This kidney desensitization experimentation is already far along. The principal pioneer is Dr. Oscar Salvatierra, chairman of the Transplant Service at the San Francisco campus of the University of California.

Dr. Salvatierra began with thirty patients who had available "related living donors," but who were considered to be extremely high risks for transplantation. Tests showed that their body defenses would immediately attack and reject the donor kidney, even though it was from a close relative.

Six weeks before each surgery, Dr. Salvatierra and his associates began a series of three small transfusions of blood from the donor into the recipient. Such "desenitization of the immune system" had worked in animals but it had never before been attempted with humans. Said Dr. Nicholas Feduska of the research team, "With our thirty patients, the results were tremendously better than anyone expected. Of the thirty high-risk patients, twenty-nine retained their transplanted new kidneys, all of which worked perfectly, with no symptoms of rejection. The one failure occurred in a patient, also a diabetic, who carelessly stopped taking his essential medication after surgery."

24

Will Gary be able to live a perfectly normal life, with marriage, children, relatively trauma-free days and nights?

There is a remarkable organization in Great Neck, New York, which is called the National Association of Patients on Hemodialysis and Transplantation, or NAPHT, for short. It refers to itself as "the voice of the kidney patient" and publishes a monthly journal, *The NAPHT News*. The journal frequently runs articles about other medical-miracle transplant recipients, all of whom provide good examples of what Gary can look forward to.

On of the most significant cases they report involves Kay and Ralph Bantz: "The significance of 3:02 A.M. January 23, 1977, shall and will be the inspiration of kidney transplant recipients the world over. A beautiful six-pound-three-ounce baby girl was born to Kay and Ralph Bantz—operative word healthy, free of any sign of kidney or any other organic impairment. 'Well, babies are born every day,' would be the natural reaction to the above statement. Adorable little Andrina is an exception to this ordinary announcement: both Mom and Dad are functioning with other human kidneys within them. To our knowledge, this is the first time in the history of the world that two people got married, both having transplants, and went on successfully to have a baby of their own.''

Until then, doctors were uncertain whether transplant patients should even consider having children. There are some hereditary factors to worry about, and pregnancy frequently puts a strain on the female kidney, even a normal one. Since the birth of Andrina Bantz, however, the taboo no longer exists. Dr. Ira Greifer reports that more than 200 normal babies have now been born to transplant patients.

The Bantz story is in many ways illuminating. Ralph was in his mid twenties and had been on dialysis for some time when a cadaver kidney became available in October 1974. The kidney was transplanted at Montefiore Hospital in New York. Ralph's body soon rejected it, however, and it was back to the dialysis machine at St. Joseph's Hospital in Yonkers, New York. But then a second donor kidney came along late in 1974. The computer came up with a good tissue match between Ralph's and this second kidney. It was transplanted, and like Gary's, it began to function while Ralph was still on the operating table.

Also, like Gary, Ralph went through one acute rejection episode, followed by some mild chronic rejection, but kidney number two has performed marvelously ever since. Ralph takes the same daily medications as Gary, Prednisone and Imuran.

In the meantime, Ralph's future wife, Kay, a lovely blonde, had been on dialysis for a year after suffering kidney disease ever since she was a small child. On November 1, 1973, she entered Montefiore Hospital for a "related living donor" kidney transplant from her sister. It was a perfect antigen match, and Kay has had no rejection problems at all, but she, too, must continue to take daily, but smaller, doses of Prednisone and Imuran.

Ralph and Kay first met on a bus going to Albany. They were both on their way to the state capital to lobby the legislature for new laws to make donor kidneys more readily available for other potential transplant recipients. Ralph and Kay continued to run into one another during their monthly checkups at Montefiore Hospital. Romance flourished amid the creatinine tests and kidney scans. They were married on Valentine's Day, February 14, 1976.

They desperately wanted to have a baby, regardless of the risks involved. Their doctors were skeptical, but finally their nephrologist, Dr. Arthur Appel, was so taken by their courage and determination that he reluctantly gave them the go-ahead. He insisted, however, that he and obstetrician Dr. Harold Schulman monitor Kay almost daily throughout the pregnancy.

There was a totally surprising lack of complications. Everything went so normally that Dr. Schulman even discarded his original plan of a Caesarean section, to lessen the risks for Kay. It was a difficult, sixteen-hour labor, but when little Andrina came into the world, both mother and infant were symptom-free, insofar as their kidneys were concerned. (According to Dr. Ira Greifer, Kay and Ralph Bantz have since had another perfect child.)

The article in *The NAPHT News* touchingly concludes: "The Bantz story expresses the hope and inspiration for men and women the world over on dialysis and as transplant recipients to keep their chins up and never think negatively, only positively. This may be a first, but think of it as a precedent for things to come for all of us in the future. Each day, medical science, God, and our own faith shall lead us to normal, productive and happy lives."

And then there's the autobiographical story of airline Captain Roger Johnson, in the November 1977, issue. Johnson begins: "It was a cold, clear, crisp afternoon on February 3, 1977, when American Airlines Flight 365 lifted off the runway at O'Hare Field in Chicago. It was to be a routine flight—except for one thing. It was the first time in history that a scheduled air-carrier aircraft was ever commanded by a kidney transplant patient. I was privileged to be the Captain of that flight."

Since Gary Coleman's admiration of railway engineers also extends to airline pilots, he is fascinated with Captain Johnson's saga.

Johnson was in his late forties, a pilot for many years, married and with five children, when his kidney disease first struck. He was hard at work remodeling the family's summer home in northern Wisconsin. Suddenly, he began to hemorrhage internally. There was excruciating pain and urine in the blood. He was rushed back home to Wheaton, Illinois, and thence to the Veterans Administration

A GIFT OF LIFE

Lakeside Hospital in Chicago. The diagnosis: polycystic kidneys. This is a birth defect which normally does not reveal itself until the mature years, when the cyst-ridden kidneys no longer can function properly. Johnson was put on a dialysis machine at the hospital and later was given a home dialysis unit. Since he couldn't fly anymore, Johnson decided to expand a small cabinet manufacturing business in northern Wisconsin which he owned with his wife, Carmen. They opted to continue living in Wheaton, since Carmen, in addition to caring for their five children, was a Spanish high school teacher and a full-time student at Wheaton College.

"So I would dialyze myself from 6 to midnight, sleep until 5 A.M." writes Johnson, "drive 340 miles to the plant in Wisconsin, work a day and a half, drive back, dialyze, and start out on the same routine again the next day."

On May 23, 1973, Johnson got a phone call from Dr. Peter Ivanovich of the Veterans Hospital. There was a cadaver kidney available. It was "a reasonably good match." Was Johnson interested? Johnson was so interested that he immediately drove the 340 miles from Wisconsin—where he had received the call—and four and a half hours later he was in the hospital and being prepared for surgery. The transplant was an unqualified success, and eleven days later, Johnson was in the auditorium at Wheaton College, watching his wife graduate with honors.

The Johnsons moved to Wisconsin, the cabinet factory prospered, but Johnson badly missed flying. He writes, "It did not take long for me to realize that I would never be satisfied until I had regained my pilot's license. After nearly thirty years of flying, one is no longer an earthbound creature. He simply cannot accept being grounded. Especially as great as I now felt. So off I went to Chicago to try to convince the U.S. Government that I was not a medical misfit."

It was a long struggle. For two years, Johnson got nowhere with the federal bureaucracies. Then Dr. H. L. Lederer, American Airlines' medical director, involved himself in the case. Dr. Lederer was knowledgeable about the advances in kidney transplantation and he wanted to see for himself how well Johnson's new kidney was working. After six months of tests, Dr. Lederer was so impressed with Johnson's condition that he recommended to the Federal Air Surgeon that Johnson could qualify for the coveted First Class Medical Certificate. He did. As Johnson writes, "It was the first one ever issued to a transplant recipient. I was not a freak after all. Now, the only stipulation is that American Airlines gives me a physical every month. And I have a government FAA physical every six months."

The end of this inspiring story is that Johnson, transplanted kidney and all, now flies a regularly scheduled California run for American Airlines.

There are numerous other such stories.

In August 1978, four young men and women with kidney transplants represented the United States in the First Transplant Olympics in Portsmouth, England. They competed in the hurdles, sprints, relays, tennis, golf, and an event called "the cricket ball throw." The American youngsters brought home no medals, but they did take fourth and fifth places against more experienced competition from Europe and Asia.

A GIFT OF LIFE

Lorraine Robertson received a cadaver transplant on December 12, 1969 in San Francisco. Today, she teaches school full time, plays vigorous tennis (with several club trophies to prove her skill and strength against normally healthy players), and she skis every winter down the most rugged slopes in the high Sierra mountains. She has made several white water rubber-raft trips down California's dangerous Rogue River. She can't believe her renewed vigor and energy since the transplant.

As a child, Donna Bingham was a severe diabetic, which ultimately resulted in kidney-damaging disease when she was a teenager. She writes, "I could no longer climb more than two or three stairs before giving out, feeling as if I would have a heart attack. My feet were swollen and it was difficult to wear shoes. I could not see well enough to read even a highway billboard."

Donna received a "related living donor" kidney transplant from her mother—after her entire family, including her brother-in-law, had volunteered to be tested as donors. One of her mother's kidneys would be the closest match, and that was the one transplanted. The mother was back at work in a matter of weeks, and Donna went on to become a registered nurse in Boston. Despite occasional periods of mild rejection of the kidney, she has prospered, unfailingly taking her drugs, which have enabled her to work toward a degree in psychology, and also to study the flute, with an eye toward playing with a local symphony orchestra in Maine. In 1978, Donna won an award as one of the Outstanding Young Women in America. She writes, "I have been able now to go back on a program of insulin and diet to keep the diabetes under control. They tell me I'm the longest surviving diabetic in the world with a kidney transplant. So each day is a gift not to be taken for granted, but to be spent doing what is really important—to live life fully as a loving, caring, giving person."

Inspirational? Indeed.

Needless to say, *The NAPHT News* also ran an article on Gary Coleman in its May 1979, issue.

25

What about Gary's growth problem?

The National Kidney Foundation's Dr. Greifer says, "One of medicine's great disappointments is that after a transplant, the children have not grown as well as expected. This is not true of all of them. Children with other forms of kidney disease do better than those with obstructive disease, which is what Gary had. To tell you the truth, we really don't know the reason why. There are many theories, but they're only theories. In any event, that's why, with the recent advances in the field, we have some new procedures we'll try, just to prolong the ability of the child's original kidney to function at a reasonable rate for as long as possible. That's to give the child a maximum chance to grow, *before* the transplant is done. So if we get a child with obstructive uropathy at age five—and that involves sixty percent of the cases in younger children—we'll do everything we can do to delay the transplant to, say, age nine or ten."

With Gary, those procedures were unknown or insufficiently tested when his obstructive uropathy was detected in 1969. In 1973, at the time of his transplant, he was three-feet-six-inches tall. In 1980, at the age of twelve, he was three-feet-ten-and-a-half inches. That's about the median height of a six-year-old.

Dr. Peter Lewy, Gary's nephrologist, says that Gary can continue to grow, but at the most, would be perhaps four-feet-eleven or five feet tall as an adult. His ultimate height will depend on many factors.

In the first place, his growth has been delayed by his illness and the steroids he is required to take in order to retain his kidney. Thus, according to Toni Greenslade, who has now become Transplant Coordinator at Children's Memorial in Chicago, Gary's so-called "bone age" is four years behind his actual chronological age. Dr. Firlit explains, "We check his wrists periodically which tells us how many years his bones have actually been growing. If he's thirteen and his bone-age is nine, that tells us his bones still have an extra four years to grow. A child normally grows until he's seventeen or eighteen. In Gary's case, with his bone-age lagging four years behind, he could continue to grow until he's twenty-one or twenty-two. You put all this data in a computer and you get a readout, but you never really know. Each child responds according to his biological needs. All we can do is adjust the steroid dosages for maximum potential growth."

But there's a second factor working in Gary's favor. Says Dr. Firlit, "That's the interesting and wonderful phenomenon called puberty. Once you go

A GIFT OF LIFE

through puberty, and the male hormone starts working, it increases metabolism and a laying on of muscle. It fuses the growth plates, and once the growth plates fuse, that launches a rapid period of growth during the adolescent period. With Gary's bone-age running well behind his chronological age, I'd predict that his puberty will be delayed until he's sixteen or seventeen. Then, we might see a sudden spurt in his height."

Dr. Griefer agrees. "Gary's not my patient, of course, but our own experience indicates that the big test for him will be when he maturates. That's the fancy word for reaching puberty. Incredible things happen at maturation, when it's delayed. I can only point to myself as an example. When I was sixteen, I was only five-feet-four. I played guard on my school basketball team. We had a center and a forward who were five-eleven. Just three years later I came back from college to visit, and I was taller than both the center and the forward. That's what late maturation can do—even, to a lesser extent, with a kidney transplant recipient."

Dr. Greifer also points out an interesting fact in the matter of bone-age vs. chronological age. "Here at the Albert Einstein Medical Center," he says, "we have kids on steroids who are thirteen years old but whose bone-age is six. We know that the minute we take them off steroids, they have all that growth to go, and some of them will jump up eight or nine inches. That's a perfectly legitimate and well-accepted medical fact." The problem is that few children can ever be taken off the steroids for very long without danger of losing the kidney to rejection.

So the doctors hypothesize while Sue and Willie Coleman hope and pray.

Sue

Along with everything else, we accepted Gary's small size as God's will. But every once in a while, something happens that gives us renewed faith. Gary *does* have little growth spurts.

It's funny, but I can always *see* them coming. It's the same every time. Gary is usually a finicky eater. Like a lot of kids, he'll turn down the fanciest meal for a hamburger, French fries and a cola. But suddenly, he'll get ravenous and eat every morsel of food we put down in front of him.

When he does that, he'll get pudgy for a time and seem to be growing sideways. Then, soon after that, the growth becomes vertical. He doesn't exactly shoot up in height, but he gets about a half-inch to an inch taller.

He had one of those spurts in 1978, and then again in 1979. We have to keep believing that when he finally reaches puberty, he'll have that *big* growth spurt the doctors keep talking about.

In the meantime, we've learned to accept the fact that even at the best, Gary is going to be shorter than most people. And it has been one big relief to me to know that Gary can deal with it and understands what he'll be facing. Sometimes, short people can be mean and overly aggressive to compensate for their lack of height, and from the very beginning Willie and I didn't want him to be that way.

So we tried. First we steered him into those areas where he could do something special he could be proud of. Then, we keep hammering away at him to accept himself the way he is, as long as he feels good about himself. He's almost there. He's really not sensitive about it anymore. Sometimes he gets aggravated. He'll complain, "Why are the cabinet doors so tall? I have to get on a chair to reach them." But he's OK and he's getting more OK all the time.

We keep reminding him of all the successful short people in the world—Paul Williams, Mickey Rooney, the Deputy Prime Minister of China, Dudley Moore, a couple of United States Senators, even some very important TV network executives. Gary's very interested in the little guys of history he learns about in school—not only Napoleon, but Alexander the Great and a lot of famous poets and philosophers.

Willie is very good in this area. My husband does a lot of bowling, for instance, and he always watches the pro bowling tour on television. Very often, when Gary is sitting there with him, I hear Willie pointing out the little guys on the tour who keep beating the big guys, and are the real geniuses of bowling.

Willie

I read up on tall guys and short guys and I talk to Gary about it all the time. Once in a while he says, "I wish I could play football," and I say,

"Why do you want to be running around in the cold with the wind blowing in your face?" I tell him most people over six-foot-one are *only* good for the physical things, like football. I tell him how I read that most of the people who do the important things in life—like being writers and artists and composers—are between four-feet-ten and five-feet-ten. You don't need stature to be on top of the world. "Look at Sammy Davis, Jr., in your own line of work," I tell him. "Look at Humphrey Bogart and James Cagney and Spencer Tracy, all those short fellows who were great actors, that you watch on TV all the time in the old movies." I tell Gary how I read once that another great actor, James Stewart, came along in the movies in the old days, and he was so tall that they thought he was a freak. Made him walk in a trench in his first picture, so he wouldn't tower over the other actors.

Gary listens when I tell him things like this, and one day, maybe, he won't pay any mind to being short at all.

If one looks at the bright side, there actually are some advantages to Gary's small size and delayed maturation. Most child actors flare briefly across the screen and then burn out. What Dr. Firlit calls "that interesting and wonderful phenomenon of puberty" occurs, and for the child actor, it isn't so wonderful—professionally, that is. The child grows up and suddenly isn't so cute anymore. According to the International Encyclopedia of film, even the greatest, Shirley Temple, "made an uneasy transition into adolescence and young womanhood, then retired from the screen after *Pride of Kentucky* (1950)."

A GIFT OF LIFE

Freddie Bartholomew, Jackie Coogan, Margaret O'Brien, Jackie Cooper, it was the same for them, though some came back much later in totally different adult personae. Elizabeth Taylor? At ten, when she made her first film, she was already a well-developed child-adult. Among the rare exceptions to make the truly successful transition were Natalie Wood, who started at three, and Mickey Rooney, who first appeared on the movie screen when he was five.

If Gary Coleman wants to continue as an actor, the peculiar medical circumstances of his delayed growth insure that he will be able to play adorable-child parts for a long time to come. After all, little Mickey Rooney still was playing Andy Hardy in films at the age of thirty-eight.

If, on the other hand, Gary wishes to move over to the executive side of the industry, he has plenty of precedents—small stature has certainly never impeded enormous success in the entertainment world. Many of the pioneers of the movie business were tiny men. Adolph Zukor was barely five feet; Louis B. Mayer and Irving Thalberg were not much taller. Even today there are many extremely small men, among them ABC movie boss Brandon Stoddard, and the brilliant film director, Arthur Hiller.

As of now, however, Gary's diminutiveness does cause him some problems, but not on the film or TV sets. At work, he's liked and respected by everyone, though there still is a tendency by all to pick him up and swing him around, or cuddle him.

The difficulties arise when he appears in public, as a celebrity. People swarm and crowd around him, and there is severe danger of his being trampled, because those beyond the first row of admirers cannot see him and keep pressing forward. He admits that such situations terrify him. "It would terrify you, too," he says, "if you had to look at the world through other people's legs."

One of the first such dangerous confrontations occurred when he and his parents were visiting his grandmother, Luretha, in Lima, Ohio. Mrs. Coleman very normally wanted to show off her grandson at the hospital where she worked. "Some folks there just didn't believe I'm Gary Coleman's grandma," she says. So Sue and Gary decided to go along with her one morning as she dropped by the hospital to pick up her paycheck.

Gary's appearance literally precipitated a mob scene. Up on the ward floors, patients—adults and children—spilled out of their beds and pushed in around him. He nearly disappeared in the crush of bodies. Panicked, Sue grabbed her son, swung him up out of harm's way, and rushed him downstairs to the lobby. It was the same there. Word had gotten around and people were piling in, even from the street, to see the star of *Diff'rent Strokes*. Holding the frightened child in her arms, well above the potentially dangerous feet of the throng, Sue could barely make her way to her car to get away from there.

It was shortly afterwards that Mr. Victor Stringer entered the life of Mr. Gary Coleman. Sue and Willie decided that in such situations, if Willie couldn't be along, Gary needed a protector-companion who would be both strong and tall. Vic Stringer is six-feet-four, 230 pounds, and with his red-bearded visage, could very well be cast as Thor in a Scandinavian folk play.

A GIFT OF LIFE

Sue, being Sue, did not cast Stringer simply because of his bulk. By that standard, any number of routine bodyguards would have sufficed. Instead, she wanted someone who was gentle and intelligent, so that he would not antagonize well-meaning but over-enthusiastic fans. Also, since he would be spending so much time with Gary when he was out of town or at public functions away from the studio, she wanted someone who would meet the boy's intellectual as well as protective needs. Stringer, a close friend of one of the Colemans' business managers, fit the bill perfectly. Not only did he have his own private-detective agency, but a master's degree in public administration from California State University at Long Beach. He was also in his second year of law school.

Stringer says, "With Gary and me, there was an initial feeling-out period. He'd look at his mother and say, 'Who *is* this guy who even has to go to the bathroom with me when I'm in a crowd?' As for me, I was uncomfortable, too. Here was a superstar, and people would stop him for autographs. He'd look to me to indicate whether he should do it or not. I had to assess each situation to determine whether or not it was threatening to him. It wasn't easy to make those judgments at first. And Gary didn't make it any easier. He just darts wherever he wants to go. He doesn't realize how small he is.

"I think the turning point came at the Emmy Awards in 1979. I always had had a thing about not picking him up because I didn't want to take away his dignity. But after the awards, there was a bad situation. People were milling around and we couldn't get out. Gary was upset. I said, 'I want you to jump up on my back and we're going to charge through this group of people. They're in our way and we have to get out of here.' "

With Gary clinging to his shoulders, Stringer charged through the throng like a fullback, and Gary rather enjoyed it. From that incident, Vic and Gary jointly developed a system whereby Gary would mount Stringer like a horse, using Stringer's hands for stirrups. He'd then ride astride Stringer's shoulders, clutching Vic's beard with both hands as if it was a set of reins.

"We do that all the time in crowds now," says Stringer. "And that led to an unusual relationship in which we play very physical games together. Like any twelve-or-thirteen-year-old, he likes to roughhouse. He'll pummel me and hit me in the belly until I make him stop by pinning his arms. When we're on the road, we'll play like that for an hour in the hotel room, while he unwinds after work. He likes to touch, but with his mother and father, it's more sitting on the lap, and kissing and hugging. The roughhousing is a special thing between Gary and me.

"The key to our relationship is that Gary's a person to me, a very special person. And the problems of his size and growth are really irrelevant."

26

In all, the word "growth"—both physical and mental—is a key element in the Gary Coleman saga, and it involves three people, not just one.

The growth of Sue and Willie is evident immediately, both in their appearance and bearing.

Willie is a nattily but conservatively dressed urbane gentleman who thinks no more of a weekend airline commute from Chicago to Los Angeles than he used to of the Saturday drives in his youth from Belzoni to Yazoo City, Mississippi. On his job, he socializes freely and easily with his white associates, especially his supervisor, Skip Randle, with whom he spends a good deal of time discussing their respective golf scores. In his dealings with Gary's business people, he is the voice of reason, a solid rock in advocating those measures he thinks are best for his son.

Willie

I care about Gary's health and I'm not going to let anyone burn him out. All he has to do for us is to stay healthy. We don't force him to do anything. The idea of being wealthy doesn't fascinate me. I'm happy just to be so much better off than I ever thought I could have been.

To me, and to everyone else, the most important thing in life is the strong family unit and the love. Without that, all these other things don't mean anything. In the worst days, when Gary was between life and death, I'd go to the storeroom at Abbott and pray there all by myself. I'd say, "Lift up your head and be proud of the wife and son you have." I still feel that way.

From what has happened to Sue, Gary and me, I know now that I was right about many things when I was a boy and I couldn't believe what my elders were trying to tell me, especially about the color of people's skin. People can be good, whether they're black, brown, tan or white. At Abbott, a man couldn't have as much support and comfort as I got from the eighty people I worked with. A couple of times I broke down and felt pulled apart, but I said to myself, "Nobody can take away from you what God has given you—with your willpower, and Gary's strength, and the prayers of all these good people."

And now, today, we have the support of good people like Vic Perillo and Harry Sloan and Larry Kuppin. They came along to guide Gary's career in the right path when nobody else would or could help us. And they made it possible for me to stay involved in Gary's career, while, at the same time, I can keep going in my own career, which a man like me has to have to be happy.

There isn't a day that I don't wake up in the morning and say, "The good Lord brought me through."

Sue, too, has come a long way from the shy country girl fresh out of Alabama. Today, she dresses with quiet elegance and she is magnificently coiffed and groomed. She has emerged as a well-spoken, beautiful young woman. While never forgetting that her first duty is to her son, she mixes easily and graciously in the more stable elements of Bel Air and Beverly Hills society. It's the same back home in Zion, with her doctor, lawyer and other successful neighbors.

Most of all, the formerly retiring Sue has become almost an evangelist for all those parents with children who are suffering from dire illnesses—and for parents in general.

Sue

Having had this experience, I now realize how important it is for people to be aware of certain things from a child's point of view. It's very different working with an adult, or taking care of an adult, than it is with a child. You also have to realize that they aren't just children. They're people. They have feelings. They have opinions. And sometimes, if you really listen to them, they come up with some pretty good ideas.

I think there are some very talented children in the world who are not given the chance to express themselves, to say what they feel, say what they want. They get sort of left out. And sometimes parents don't realize that when a child is always mouthing off, they say, "Oh, be quiet. I get tired of listening to you." But if you listen to that child, sometimes extremely intelligent things come out of their mouths. It shocks you sometimes. You turn around and ask, "What did you say?"

There are promising and just sort of overlooked kids out there. Especially the poor kids. The kids who come from rich families don't miss much because they have the opportunity. But the children from the ghettos who can sit down and write a poem, who can remember things they have read and have photographic memories —these are the children who are overlooked. And when they're sick, you should listen, because they're so bright they might know more about their illness than you do.

Sometimes they get especially independent when they're ill, only to get squelched by the parents who are being overprotective. Once, for example, Gary came into the kitchen and said, "What are you cooking? Can I do that?" Well, cooking is a form of creativity, too, so we let him do it. Gary cooked a full meal for his daddy and me. We sat and watched television while he played cook. He made hamburgers, French fries, salad—and the works. He served it, and we ate it, and he bragged that he cooked better than his mother. But he's expressing himself, and you have to say, "OK, I know he's going to mess up my kitchen, I know it's going to be a disaster area, but I have to let him do it because even this helps to make him feel important."

When a child is sick, you sometimes must say, "You have to get up and walk." The child will say, "I can't. I don't want to." But you must get him on his feet and then you say, "OK, I'm going to hold you, and then I'm going to turn you loose." And you turn him loose and let him go on his own. Maybe it's the hardest thing you've ever done in your life, but you have to let them do it. They have to grow. They have to be independent. They have to be able to feel for themselves, to feel inside of them.

In the same way, we always have sort of sat down with Gary and said, "Well, what do you think about this, or what do you think about that?" We can talk about politics, and Gary has some very strong opinions, which he will not hesitate to voice. And you have to listen to him, because if you don't, that's depressing him; it's pushing him back if you don't listen to what he's got to say.

It makes us stop and think when he comes up with ideas like "I think this country would be much better off if we just got rid of everything and went back to the barter system. Then nobody would have more than the other person. It's not fair for some people to have everything and other people not to have anything."

So we let him talk, and we listen, which is most

important of all for children who have a chronic condition like his. It's so easy for them to get into a rut. They think, "I'm never going to be any good. All I can do is sit here and feel sorry for myself." It's up to you to make them realize that that's not the way it is. They have to be independent. They have to have something that *they* can do. The potential is always there for *something*, and you must encourage them. If someone doesn't say, "You can do it," they won't do it.

That's why I hope our experience somehow can be helpful to other parents who have children with similar conditions, people who are going through similar problems, either mental or physical. I hope those parents can learn from how we did it. I hope those children can look at Gary and realize he's a fighter; he wants something and goes after it.

Nothing would make me happier than for some of those children to say, "Well, if Gary Coleman can do it, then there's no reason why *I* can't do it."

27

All the Coleman growth elements were dramatically evident one warm summer afternoon in Chicago in 1980. It was Saturday, June 28, near the end of filming *On the Right Track*, Gary's first big theatrical movie for 20th Century-Fox distribution. It was about a young orphan, a horse-race-betting genius, who lives in a baggage locker in Chicago's Union Station.

On that Saturday, as on most days of the production schedule, filming was taking place in the venerable old train terminal itself.

Gary

It was a pretty wild day. Mostly we didn't shoot on Saturdays, but there had been a lot of trouble and we were trying to catch up. During the week, we had to get out of the way when the rush hours started and the station was filled with people running to catch trains. On Saturday, there wasn't so much people. I remember that one Saturday very well.

Our production headquarters was set up in the big old fancy restaurant in the station. They don't use this restaurant anymore. In the old days, it was the place where rich people hung out when they traveled coast to coast by train, and they had to wait a few hours between the time when the Twentieth Century Limited came in from New York and the Santa Fe Super Chief left for L.A.

Both Mom and Dad were very busy in this big old empty restaurant on that Saturday. Mom was on the phone a lot, sitting in one of the red leather booths where the leather was cracked and someone had stuck it together again with black tape. She was making the arrangements for me to appear at a big function in Gary, Indiana, the next week. The National Kidney Foundation was gonna get a pledge of a lot of money from the United Steelworkers union, and they wanted me there to say a few words and thank the steelworkers. I listened to Mom making the arrangements for me on the phone, and I was proud of how she was handling it. She sounded like she had been doing this kind of public relations work all her life.

At the other end of the empty old restaurant, Dad was at another ratty table talking to Harry Sloan and Larry Kuppin. There had been a big flap on the set the day before and Dad had been called down from Zion to help straighten it out. What happened was that the director, Lee Phillips, got into a fight with one of the production people, and he said he was walking off the picture and wouldn't show up for work that morning.

Larry Sloan had been there when the flap happened. He got on the phone to ask Dad to drive down from Zion, and he also asked Larry Kuppin to fly in from Los Angeles. They met in the middle of the night with Lee Phillips and the guy he was fighting with, and they worked out an agreement at about two-thirty in the morning so that Lee would go to work in the morning, which he did. Larry told me Dad had played a very important part in these delicate negotiations. As I watched Dad, still working out the last details there in the restaurant, I sure was proud of him.

I didn't have much to do that morning. They were shooting a lot of other people on one of the train platforms, and I only had to be with them in a few of the scenes. So I snuck across a couple of tracks to have a look at one of the new Superliner double-decker passenger cars. A conductor saw me looking, and he let me go in to see the inside of the cars. He explained that these cars were the greatest, but that they were so tall they couldn't be used on any tracks where they had to go through tunnels.

As usual, Vic Stringer was glued to me wherever I went. I tried to give him a few shots in the belly and wrestle with him, but he pinned my arms, like he always seems able to do. I ran around the station a lot, with him following me. I spent some of my spare time playing electronic games in the pinball machine arcade. Wherever I went in the station, there were a lot of people, especially kids, who kept calling me by name and walking around behind me, and asking me to autograph things like train schedules, which I did.

We broke for lunch late that day, about three o'clock. Vic made his hands into a stirrup and I stepped in them with my left foot and climbed up onto his big shoulders, like he was a horse. He then pushed through the crowds, with me up there on his shoulders, and we headed for the Cafe Bohemia to go eat.

About a dozen kids kept trailing along behind us, watching me riding up there about eight feet in the air. One of the kids was about fourteen years old, and he was very small, and he looked kinda sad as he ran along looking up there at me. The kid said, "Hey, Gary, how does it feel to be a tall guy?"

I looked down at him and I said, "Hey, man, there's an awful lot of short guys out there who people of all sizes look up to."

Vic turned his big old head around and said, "Now where did you get *that* one from?"

I said, "From Ann Landers' column."

Everybody laughed.

I like to make people laugh.

Glittering lives of famous people!
Bestsellers from Berkley

✯✯✯✯✯✯✯✯✯✯✯✯✯✯✯✯✯✯✯✯✯✯✯✯✯

___	**MISS TALLULAH BANKHEAD** Lee Israel	04574-9—$2.75
___	**BRANDO FOR BREAKFAST** Anna Kashfi Brando and E.P. Stein	04698-2—$2.75
___	**GARY COLEMEN: A GIFT OF LIFE** The Coleman Family and Bill Davidson	05595-7—$2.95
___	**CONVERSATIONS WITH JOAN CRAWFORD** Roy Newquist	05046-7—$2.50
___	**FRANCES FARMER: SHADOWLAND** William Arnold	05481-0—$2.75
___	**SUSAN HAYWARD: PORTRAIT OF A SURVIVOR** Beverly Linet	05030-0—$2.95
___	**RITA HAYWORTH: THE TIME, THE PLACE AND THE WOMAN** John Kobal	05634-1—$2.95
___	**HOLLYWOOD IN A SUITCASE** Sammy Davis, Jr.	05091-2—$2.95
___	**LADD: A HOLLYWOOD TRAGEDY** Bevery Linet	05731-3—$2.95
___	**MOMMIE DEAREST** Christina Crawford	05242-7—$3.25
___	**MOTHER GODDAM** Whitney Stine with Betty Davis	05394-6—$2.95
___	**MY WICKED, WICKED WAYS** Errol Flynn	04686-9—$2.75
___	**NO BED OF ROSES** Joan Fontaine	05028-9—$2.75
___	**SELF-PORTRAIT** Gene Tierney with Micky Herskowitz	04485-8—$2.75
___	**SHOW PEOPLE** Kenneth Tynan	04750-4—$2.95
___	**TRUE BRITT** Britt Ekland	05341-5—$2.95

Berkley Book Mailing Service
P.O. Box 690
Rockville Centre, NY 11570

Please send me the above titles. I am enclosing $_____
(Please add 50¢ per copy to cover postage and handling). Send check or money order—no cash or C.O.D.'s. Allow six weeks for delivery.

NAME_____

ADDRESS_____

CITY_____ STATE/ZIP_____

6Au

MS READ-a-thon— a simple way to start youngsters reading

Boys and girls between 6 and 14 can join the MS READ-a-thon and help find a cure for Multiple Sclerosis by reading books. And they get two rewards — the enjoyment of reading, and the great feeling that comes from helping others.

Parents and educators: For complete information call your local MS chapter. Or mail the coupon below.

Kids can help, too!

Mail to:
National Multiple Sclerosis Society
205 East 42nd Street
New York, N.Y. 10017

I would like more information about the MS READ-a-thon and how it can work in my area.

MS Mystery Sleuth

Name _____
(please print)
Address _____
City _____ State _____ Zip _____
Organization _____